Python Machine Learning

Python for beginners to learn new techniques complete guide for data analytics to learn computer programming how to master python for data science

Tony F. Charles

Table of Contents

Introduction

The world continues to advance every day. Every now and then, we find humanity discovering newer realms and expanding the horizon far beyond what we once thought possible. That is the magic of science. However, this entire feat was probably not possible without the invention of computer programming languages. Every major success we have had in terms of technology comes from some form of computer programming.

Today, the world is awash with programming languages such as the R, C# (called C Sharp), JavaScript, the list is just endless. While we continue to search for new languages to further explore new possibilities, one language stands out for its sheer effectiveness, simplicity and exceptional use in the world of today. Created by Guido Van Rossum, Python has become a new benchmark for beginners and experts alike.

Leading platforms around the world are using Python as their core programming language. Whether we speak about social media giants such as Instagram, or the latest radar-guided and satellite-guided self-driven cars, Python is found to be in the heart of the entire success. It is because of Python that the world has now taken an interest in Data Science and Machine learning, the two leading frontiers of technology.

Naturally, it makes great sense for any programmer to seek guidance to learn and master the technicalities involved behind these two, which is where this book will step in.

Unlike many other books, we will jump straight to the good bits and keep it true to the "clean code writing" practice as possible. You will get ample explanation only where they may be required; the rest are self-explanatory by nature.

What exactly is machine learning? While the book talks about the more advanced aspects of machine learning, here's a little explanation for anyone who is thinking about taking up Machine Learning as their choice of field.

Generally speaking, we human beings learn from our past experiences and correct our headings to ensure the results we desire are obtained. Machines, on the other hand, are programmed by us, without the option of allowing them to learn from their past experiences. With Machine Learning, we now have the option to allow the machines to learn from their past experiences. Sure enough, the machine cannot do anything unless we allow it to carry out a specific task. In this case, we will become the trainer and the machines will become the students. We will use this book to have a look into what are some advanced ways to ensure that we train our machine, test out their capabilities, check their accuracy and quite a lot more.

The idea to write a book with practical codes is one that has been taken up by quite a lot of esteemed authors and publishers, however, this book was created to ensure a good chunk of such codes and variations were used. We will encounter quite a few terminologies that may seem daunting at first, but the explanations provided should be easy to understand.

Python Machine Learning is a book that ensures all technicalities are catered and applied to examples to showcase their unique features and differences. Through carefully created codes and snippets, it would be easy to draw a conclusion and learn a thing or two about the various methods used within this book.

While there are quite a few graphs that were omitted, owing to the fact that these were almost identical in nature, readers are encouraged to try to manipulate the data to see the minor yet existing differences.

To get the most out of this book, there is only one thing you can do: Practice. The more you practice your coding skills, the better you learn and understand matters. In the interest of advanced learning, we will not be visiting any basics but instead will be focusing on advanced terminologies, methods, and their usages only.

If you have just started using Python, it is best that you create a good understanding of how to code with Python before embarking on a journey to the world of Machine learning.

Who should read this book?

This book ideally aims to provide a learning experience to professionals who are practicing machine learning tools to investigate real-world issues. This book is an advanced level of learning and requires some basic knowledge of machine learning and artificial intelligence (AI). There is quite a lot of software that can be used for applying machine learning algorithms, but we will focus on using Python along with a few selected software's and libraries. It is understood that by reading this book, you have a basic understanding of what libraries are and how they are used in python for algorithm development. You must be familiar with the basics of NumPy, Matplotlib and Scikit-learn as these will be our primary sources to work with.

If you have yet to come across these libraries and software's, it is probably best to acquire the required knowledge first prior to reading the content within this book. While there is no harm in doing so, there is a good possibility that you might be overwhelmed with commands, functions, libraries, and other methods used within the book if you have never used them before.

There will be times where you might feel overwhelmed by the sheer number of codes used within this book. If you are not sure about some of these, you can always browse the internet to gain a better perspective. These codes were designed with specific datasets and hence some functions, methods and parameters were used that were related to these codes. For a list of complete methods and functions, be sure to visit websites pertaining to said libraries to find a list of these. We will not be going through all of them within this book.

Before you do go ahead and start your journey, it is essential to know that you will need to use the latest version of Python on your system. It does not matter whether you are using Windows, Macintosh OS or any distribution of Linux, the coding will remain universal. However, having Python-2 will surely have a few troubles. Therefore, it is essential that you use Python-3.x.x (whichever is applicable) to follow the book without encountering any errors.

Purpose of this book

There are many books written on python and machine learning. It is only natural that you might be asking how is this book any different. Most of these books either dive deep into theories behind python and machine learning unnecessarily or gave simple generic examples consisting of general problems. This book deals with only real-world problems and applies almost all methods of machine learning to make you gain a better understanding of algorithms and provide you with a practical way to resolve and investigate real-world issues.

At the end of reading this book, you will be able to compare all methods of machine learning and ready to apply these algorithms both efficiently and effectively. This book is to be taken as a reference book and does not necessarily guarantee that the content shown here would work on future versions of the language or software's used. All commands, libraries, coding methods used here were valid at the time of writing this book. If you run into such issues where certain methods, functions or commands no longer work, use the Python community to seek answers.

Python is one of the most well-documented languages in existence that allows you to learn almost everything about the language by scrolling through the community forums. You are encouraged to take advantage of it when and where possible to help you further accelerate your learning.

It is imperative that you understand that we will be using Anaconda as our prime environment for development purposes as it contains all the necessary packages and libraries that we need in order to try out, test, and learn machine learning. The datasets used within the book are predefined and available within Scikit-Learn. Should you find yourself in a spot of trouble, you can always search for those online to find out how to access them.

The Python version in use throughout the book will be 3.x.x as Python 2 is slightly different and will run out of services soon. If you do not have Python 3 installed, head over to www.python.org to download the latest version of Python 3.

Although the book provides various examples and data visualizations, it is not to be taken as the only guide to learn from. This book covers all the bases of Machine Learning and puts various methods to use with numerous scenarios. You can visit online repositories to gain access to all of these datasets and libraries. Use this book as your reference, and aim to learn and develop a sound understanding of matters involved in machine learning. By the end of this book, we aim to allow a student or an aspirant to have enough confidence to carry out various experiments using their own imaginations, scenarios and codes.

If you encounter errors during the process of executing codes or during the installation of any of the libraries, software or plugins, ensure to visit the concerned websites or ask the ever-active community of Python programmers and Machine learners on various platforms.

All the codes written were tried and tested during the writing of this book. All of these were found to be working and result-oriented. However, it is not to be taken for granted that these codes will work perfectly in future releases of any of the components involved.

Lastly, the book was written after thorough research and wishes to provide more practical coding than theory. Should you feel overwhelmed at any point, stop and take a bit of a break. Do not try and pace through the lines. Sometimes, a glass of water and some fresh air might be just what you need to get you back into the productive zone.

Take this book as your ultimate reference book and extract as much knowledge from this book as possible. Always remember that you can and will encounter errors. There is nothing to be alarmed about any of those as these errors will not affect or jeopardize your system as a whole. Upon encountering an error, debug the code and correct the values, parameters or arguments to ensure the code is able to work perfectly.

Chapter 1: Getting Started With Machine Learning

Machine learning is a method that is used to get information from the given data sets. These data sets are then used to train systems using the provided information so that they can be used to provide output of corresponding input when any input is given. It has numerous applications. Although it can be used for both small and sizeable data, usually it is mainly used to process a high quantity of data in quick time and then return the output in relation to the input provided.

Machine learning is what allows AI to gain the ability to self-learn and improve itself through various occurrences and experiences. There is a reason that this field has quickly garnered quite a lot of attention from the rest of the world. More and more people are now willing to learn Python to understand Machine Learning and be able to write and execute programs that can further enable their AIs to become intelligent systems.

We already have an example of how this sublime technology is being used in weather systems. Through carefully designed architectures and programs, the system now has the ability to comprehend, understand and then predict what the weather conditions will be like in the coming days. This is made possible through effective use of AI. Take the machine learning away, and we might be back to computing individual variables and data for hours before realizing that the results are in a little too late.

What is Machine Learning?

By now, you may have already acquired an idea as to what machine learning is. It is an efficient way to process large quantities of data in the smallest amount of time and allow systems to gain the ability to learn from the given data. It is used to provide prediction of future values by training itself with current and old values. It is used in many cases these days such as the automatic recommendation regarding best movies, ordering the best food, and buying the best products.

Similarly, it is used to recognize your friends in photos stored on Facebook and other social platforms through facial recognition. It is also used in platforms such as Amazon and Netflix. Hence, machine learning can be used in many ways, and that is precisely why it is necessary to gain an understanding at an advanced level so that it can be used to solve multiple problems and deliver various services to ease the users further.

In the old days, "if and else" statements were used for processing of data or adjusting user input in order to make intelligent applications. There was a spam filter that was used to transfer specific emails to spam folder. How do you think this was done with emails to categorize them as spam?

Spam filter used a list of blacklisted words that helped the filter to identify spam. This filter can be used as one of the examples of intelligent applications. This problem can be solved by a human as well, but in that case, a person requires enough understanding of processes to come up with such a model. Manual or hand-coded rules can be useful but not in every case, as mentioned above. It can have some disadvantages as follows:

· The code or system will work for a specific problem; any change in the problem can lead to failure of that code or system.

· A human being may not be able to develop such a thorough understanding quickly and might consume quite a lot of time to carry out such work.

Similarly, there is one more example in which the hand-coded method fails, and that is the detection of a face in an image. Although every smartphone these days can detect and identify faces in the pictures, these were not identified successfully in the past. The reason behind failure in detection and identification of faces in an image in the recent past is the difference in perception of pixels between a human and a computer.

Computer perceives images differently as compared to humans. The improvement from failure to success in detection of a face in an image is due to the utilization of machine learning algorithms. The machine learning-based program contains large samples of pictures, which is enough to detect and identify various faces within an image.

Types of learning and their examples

Just a few minutes ago, we discussed the use of spam filters within our emails and how it transfers individual emails to our junk mail folder while retaining the others in the inbox. The machine learning algorithm can perform this work efficiently. All it requires is a sample of spam words or emails for the training of the model, and then that model will categorize spam emails. In reality, that model will predict emails as spam or otherwise.

The model that requires training needs machine learning. Furthermore, the selection of methods depends on the situation of the problem at hand.

If the problem provides the information of categorization as an input, it is known as **supervised learning**. On the other hand, if the problem does not provide the information of categorization as an input, it is known as **unsupervised learning**. Clustering is a perfect example of unsupervised learning, while classification and regression are examples of supervised learning.

The term 'Supervised' learning is recognized from the term supervision, just as a teacher supervises his/her students on a specific task and guides them regarding inputs and outputs. In doing this, they learn the sequence of that particular problem.

Likewise, supervised learning takes inputs and learns its outputs as well, and when other data is given to it, it can predict its output using the trained model.

Supervised learning can further be explained, and to do that, let us assume another example situation. Suppose that you are presented with three similar pills of the same dimensions and all are of the same color.

- Pill A - five grams
- Pill B - six grams
- Pill C - 7 grams

We have the weights. Here, the weight will turn into a component called 'feature,' which we will be using shortly to classify these. Let us assume that we have another data that is already defined in the machine. The machine will cross-check with the data and immediately recognize these pills based on their 'features' and provide them with their names. Names are defined as labels. Your end result may look like this:

- (name of drug) - 5 grams
- (name of drug) - 6 grams
- (name of drug) - 7 grams

Here, the name of the drug can be anything that is predefined. The same can be used to identify coins, metals, ornaments, and objects.

In the above example, we have features and the machine uses labeled data to identify these and provide outputs accordingly.

On the other hand, unsupervised learning has no awareness of outputs to specific inputs, and when a different data set is given, it can just categorize outputs on the basis of some parameters such as Euclidean distance, etc. To put it in plain terms, unsupervised data works on unlabeled data and provides outputs in cluster forms.

We will see some more examples of both supervised learning and unsupervised learning to develop a better understanding of these schemes. One of the most common examples of supervised learning is the identification of zip codes from handwritten digits on an envelope.

In this example, you have scans of handwriting as input, and zip code is the desired output. You need to collect multiple envelopes to create datasets for the training model. Hence, when any handwritten digits are provided to the system as an input, the algorithm will provide the zip codes as output.

Another example of supervised learning is determining whether the tumor is benign in a medical image. Here, you have the medical images as input, and the desired output will inform whether the tumor is benign or not. You would need to collect multiple medical images to make datasets for the training model. Hence, when any medical image is fed to the system as an input, the algorithm will come into play and inform regarding the intensity of the said tumor. Machine learning is used quite often in the field of medical imaging.

To quote yet another example of supervised learning, it is the detection of fraudulent activity in the transactions of credit cards. Following the same pattern as above, you have credit card transactions as input, and the output will determine whether the said transaction is legitimate or fraudulent in nature. Once again, you will need to collect credit card transactions to make datasets for the training model. Hence, when any credit card transactions are fed to the system as inputs, the algorithm will produce the results accordingly.

With a bit of an understanding of how supervised learning works, let us now look at some examples of unsupervised learning. One of the examples of unsupervised learning is the identification of topics in blog posts.

The large number of textual data that you have represents these blog posts as input, and you want to summarize the themes of these posts. Since you don't know about these topics, the outputs are unknown. Hence, without any known corresponding outputs of these inputs, you need to summarize the themes of these posts. This can pose a bit of a challenge as you will need to rely on other methods to gather the related information and categorize them accordingly. See how supervised learning is much more efficient?

Another example of unsupervised learning is the segmentation of customers into groups with similarities. In this example, you have a massive number of customer records as input, and you want to identify which customers have similarities.

Customers can be parents, book buyers or gamers. You don't know about these groups, and naturally the output is unknown. Hence, without any known corresponding outputs of these inputs, you need to identify similarities among customers and then segment them on the basis of those similarities on your own.

Finally, we have an example of unsupervised learning for the detection of abnormal access patterns to websites. Here, you have a large number of website access records as input and you want to identify which access is classified as abnormal. The abnormal accesses will be different from each other. Since you have no idea about these accesses and how they are organized, the outputs are unknown. Therefore, without any known corresponding outputs of these inputs, you now need to identify which access is abnormal on your own.

By no means are we stating that of these two methods only one is usable. There are cases where both can be used, depending on the input and output of the scenario. However, as the book progresses, you will soon learn why the former is favored over the latter.

Now that we have seen a few examples where Machine Learning is applied, let us now shift our attention to the more technical aspects, one where we start setting up our environment, gathering the right tools and starting our own venture.

Installing Machine Libraries in Your System

Before we commence, the readers are reminded that this book is meant for intermediate to advanced users, which is why we will not be explaining the basic terminologies involved in Python and programming in general, such as libraries, classes, arrays, lists, tuples and so on.

There are multiple libraries that are required to be installed in Python in order to apply Machine learning. Some of them are basic libraries, while some are more advanced in nature. Each library has its own usage. These are usually used for performing specific operations.

First, we have Scikit-learn. Scikit-learn is a free-to-use package, hence it is also known as an open-source package. It is being developed much throughout the world, and it is being used by many programmers. It is quite a great package, and almost every advanced program should be able to recognize it.

It contains many Machine learning-based algorithms. This package relies on other two packages of Python; SciPy and NumPy. Furthermore, you will need to install additional packages of Python, such as matplotlib for plotting, and Jupyter Notebook for development.

There are some distributions of Python that automatically install some packages when installed. Anaconda is one of them. It is used for large-scale processing of data, scientific computing, and analyzing of prediction. It automatically installs Scipy, NumPy, pandas, matplotlib, Jupyter Notebook, IPython, and Scikit-learn.

Enthought Canopy is another distribution of Python, which is usually used for scientific computing. It automatically installs Scipy, NumPy, pandas, matplotlib, IPython, and Jupyter Notebook. However, it does not automatically install the Scikit-learn package, especially with the free version.

Python (x,y) is another distribution of Python, which is also used for scientific computing. It is a free version. It automatically installs Scipy, NumPy, pandas, matplotlib, IPython, and Scikit-learn. If you have installed Python, you need to use pip command to install all of the above mentioned package.

$ pip install scipy numpy matplotlib pandas ipython scikit-learn

Once done, we are ready to proceed to the next step.

How to import libraries

To import libraries and verify their versions, run the following line of codes:

Input:

import sys

print("Version of Python: {}".format(sys.version))

Output:

> Version of Python: 3.6.5 |Anaconda, Inc.| (default, Mar 29 2018, 13:32:41) [MSC v.1900 64 bit (AMD64)]

In order to import pandas:

Input:

import pandas as pd

print("Version of pandas: {}".format(pd.__version__))

Output:

Version of pandas: 0.23.0

In order to import matplotlib:

Input:

import matplotlib

print("Version of matplotlib: {}".format(matplotlib.__version__))

Output:

Version of matplotlib: 2.2.2

In order to import SciPy:

Input:

import scipy as sp

print("Version of scipy: {}".format(sp.__version__))

Output:

Version of scipy: 1.1.0

And then for the rest:

Input:

import IPython

print("Version of IPython: {}".format(IPython.__version__))

Output:

Version of IPython: 6.4.0

Input:

import sklearn

print("Version of sklearn: {}".format(sklearn.__version__))

Output:

Version of sklearn: 0.19.1

You may have noticed that we are always demanding the console to print out the version information. This part is to ensure that we know which versions we are using as some of these commands may stop working in future releases.

We are all set to move toward our next chapter. This is where we will learn in detail about supervised learning and how we can apply it in various circumstances.

Chapter 2: Supervised Machine Learning for Discrete Class Label

Supervised learning holds quite a significance in the field of Machine Learning. We can already sense a feeling that the word 'supervised' has something to do with supervision. It is just as a teacher would teach and guide students about which inputs can provide outputs of desired types. But, when we mention supervised learning, you will come across another term that tags along with supervised learning: Classification.

Understanding the Concept of Classification

Supervised machine learning is divided into two types, classification, and regression. Classification is used to predict discrete labels. It is further divided into two categories, binary classification and multi-classification. Binary classification is used to divide two classes while multi-classification is used to separate multiple classes. We can safely say that binary classification yields us either a yes or a no. We discussed the example of classification of emails as either spam or not in the previous chapter as an example. That example relates to the binary classification.

On the other hand, regression is used to predict continuous numbers or floating-point numbers. Its examples are: prediction of an individual's annual income from his/her education, age, and residence. While predicting annual income, the predicted output will be an amount that will be of any value. Similarly, predicting the yield of a cornfield by providing number of features such as previous yields, weather, and the number of employees allocated on that farm is an example of regression. The predicted output can be any number.

It is very important to distinguish between classification and regression. You can distinguish between these two terms by figuring out whether predicted output contains any continuity or not; if yes, then it is an example of regression. In the example of the annual income of individuals, you can see how it is an example of regression.

Suppose you need to translate the language of any website, you can translate that language completely with a single click. This is an example of classification.

Overfitting and underfitting

While training datasets, you need to take care of some of the factors. Assuming that you are training datasets to make a model. You are sure that your dataset or model will work on your test data, but will that model work on a new test data? Are you quite sure about it? Will you need to completely change the model to work for other test data?

To explain further, let us take this statement as an example:

"People older than 40 want to buy a boat."

This statement can explain the behavior of all the customers; you know you just need to create a threshold of 40. Any other person that has an age of less than 40 will be considered as not willing to buy a boat. But on the other hand, you cannot simply tell any simple rule for this problem at first look. If you make a very complex model that will work for that specific problem, and it fills too closely to that specific problem, it is called overfitting. On the flip side, if you make a very simple model that is not taking care of all aspects of data, your model will neither work for the test data nor will it work effectively for the training set as well. This problem is called underfitting.

The reason behind these errors is that with making complex models, you allow your model to perform well on training data. But when you create too complex of a model, you force yourself to think more and more and in return you come up with taking care of each and every data point, and that might be counterproductive. Although that model will work on your training data but it will not work with new data. Similarly, a model that is too simple leads us to failure in prediction. You need to trade-off between overfitting and underfitting to get the right balance and get the optimum output.

Along with these factors, you need to keep in mind the time required in simulation of any algorithm. The more complex you create your algorithms, the more time it will consume for simulation. Sometimes, we are bound by time limits and require quicker results, and in such cases, we need to keep our algorithms simple. We will encounter all these factors while performing classification methods. It is recommended that you try out executing the programs and methods with numerous values. It is a good practice to develop an understanding.

Machine Learning Methods

K-Nearest Neighbors

Suppose you have an individual profile and you have successfully gathered some data pertaining to the liking and disliking of a person for movies. Based on the data we have gathered, let us assume the following situations:

- Mr. A loves to watch horror movies
- Mr. A prefers watching movies based on Science Fiction
- Mr. A dislikes watching romance films
- Mr. A prefers watching movies based on true stories
- Mr. A watches movies that are 90 minutes long

Now we have some general data, and if we map these values on a graph, where the x-axis represents genres and the y-axis represents the runtime of the film, we can easily visualize the data. So far, so good.

Let us bring a little technicality in this mix. Suppose there is a new movie out that is around 100 minutes long, and it is an action movie. This will now pose a problem for us.

In the initial data that has been gathered, there is no mention of the word 'action' and we already have a 90 minutes runtime mark established. Will Mr. A like this movie? This is where the K-Nearest Neighbors method comes into play.

It is the simplest machine learning algorithm to be used for the classification process. It has become a very popular machine learning algorithm for both classification and regression processes. It takes K nearest neighbors (KNN) to calculate a new data point for a given data. If the value of k is one, then it will be in its simplest form, which will take only one nearest neighbor to calculate a new data point from a given data. It will operate the same way for calculating new data points for all the given data.

To put things in the simplest words, the KNN method will take into consideration the nearest data points and gauge the majority. If the model sees that similar items are more in number compared to the ones that Mr. A dislikes, it will end up recommending this movie to Mr. A. Quite similar to how we see recommendations on YouTube, Netflix, and other streaming platforms.

Now, let us dive in a little deeper into the technicalities and see how KNN works with datasets. We will apply KNN on both Iris and Breast cancer datasets to perform classification process and we will then check its performance.

Applying KNN on Breast cancer dataset

Let us see how KNN works with a relatable example, as shown under:

Input:

Importing required libraries

from sklearn.datasets import load_breast_cancer as cancer

from sklearn.neighbors import KNeighborsClassifier as KNN

import matplotlib.pyplot as plt

Loading input data

```python
value = cancer()

Data = value.data

Target = value.target


# Splitting input data into training and testing data

ts = len(Data)

trs = round(0.7*ts) #You can change this partition and the
remainder will be for testing

Data_trn = Data[0: trs]

Target_trn = Target[0: trs]


Data_tst = Data[trs:]

Target_tst = Target[trs:]


# Printing size of training and testing data

print(Data_trn.shape)
```

```
print(Data_tst.shape)
```

Output:

(398, 30)

(171, 30)

Input:

```
accuracy_trn = []
accuracy_tst = []


limit = range(1, 11)
for i in limit:

        # Training the model

        knn = KNN(n_neighbors = 2)

        knn.fit(Data_trn, Target_trn)

        # Calculating accuracy of Training Data

    accuracy_trn.append(knn.score(Data_trn, Target_trn))

        # Calculating accuracy of Testing Data
```

accuracy_tst.append(knn.score(Data_tst, Target_tst))

Plotting accuracy of training and testing data

plt.plot(limit, accuracy_trn, label = "Accuracy of Training Data")

plt.plot(limit, accuracy_tst, label = "Accuracy of Testing Data")

plt.xlabel("Value")

plt.ylabel("Accuracy")

plt.legend()

Output:

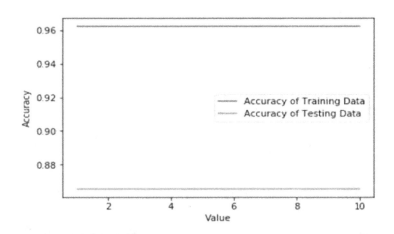

Accuracies of training and testing on Breast cancer dataset
using KNN with 2 neighbors without split command

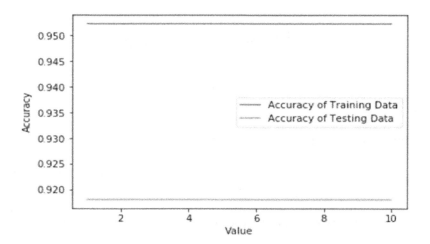

Accuracies of training and testing on Breast cancer dataset using KNN with 3 neighbors without split command

By change in value of n_neighbors (representing the number of neighbors) from 2 to 3 in the below-mentioned command, you can observe the increase in accuracy of the KNN algorithm. As with the increase in the value of the nearest neighbors, the accuracy of the KNN algorithm increases. But by increasing too many nearest neighbors, the complexity, and simulation time will be increased as well.

knn = KNN(n_neighbors = 2)

You need to change parameters of algorithms to check their performances. You can change number of neighbors. Can you change it to 10? Why not try it out yourself? What do you suppose the output will be? Will it change the accuracy?

Currently, this example is using 70% of data for training and 30% data for testing. Try and change the partition to 50% each and see what the results are. You can do that by altering the value in "trs = round(0.7 * ts)". Remember, the percentage you use here will automatically assign the remainder to the testing data. Check the results by changing these values for the testing data. You will notice how the changes take effect.

It is to be kept in mind that 70-30 partition is only applicable in this specific dataset. It is a good likelihood that this might not work in other cases. Therefore, we will now look at how to deal with such cases the split command.

Applying KNN on Breast cancer dataset with the split command

Input:

```
# Importing required libraries

from sklearn.datasets import load_breast_cancer as cancer

from sklearn.neighbors import KNeighborsClassifier as KNN

from sklearn.model_selection import train_test_split as tss

import matplotlib.pyplot as plt


# Loading input data

value = cancer()


# Splitting input data into training and testing data

Data_trn, Data_tst, Target_trn, Target_tst = tss(value.data,
value.target, random_state=10)


# Printing size of training and testing data
```

```
print(Data_trn.shape)

print(Data_tst.shape)
```

Output:

```
 (426, 30)

(143, 30)
```

Input:

```
accuracy_trn = []

accuracy_tst = []


limit = range(1, 11)

for i in limit:

        # Training the model

   knn = KNN(n_neighbors = 2)

        knn.fit(Data_trn, Target_trn)

        # Calculating accuracy of Training Data

        accuracy_trn.append(knn.score(Data_trn, Target_trn))
```

Calculating accuracy of Testing Data

accuracy_tst.append(knn.score(Data_tst, Target_tst))

Plotting accuracy of training and testing data

plt.plot(limit, accuracy_trn, label = "Accuracy of Training Data")

plt.plot(limit, accuracy_tst, label = "Accuracy of Testing Data")

plt.xlabel("Value")

plt.ylabel("Accuracy")

plt.legend()

Output:

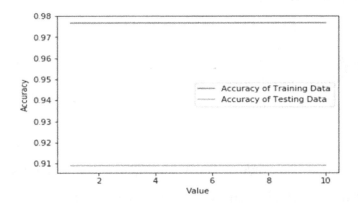

Accuracies of training and testing on Breast cancer dataset
using KNN with 2 neighbors with split command

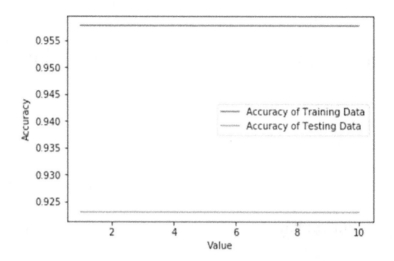

Accuracies of training and testing on Breast cancer dataset using KNN with 3 neighbors with split command

Again, you can observe that by changing the value of n_neighbors from 2 to 3 in the below-mentioned command, accuracy of KNN algorithm will increase.

```
knn = KNN(n_neighbors = 2)
```

Play with this code again. Try to change the parameters of algorithms to check their performances. Can you change number of neighbors to 5? What output will you get now? Will it change the accuracy? Remember, through trial and error, we get to learn a lot. Do not be overwhelmed by any error you might encounter as this is a part of the learning.

Decision Tree

The decision tree method is another example of machine learning, which is used for both classification and regression processes. They work on making trees based on decisions to classify the datasets. This method contains if and else statements. The tree starts with data points having maximum probability among others. It makes multiple trees that are connected with each other. We will apply Decision tree on both Iris and Breast cancer datasets to perform classification process and then we will check its performance in terms of accuracy.

Applying Decision Tree on Breast cancer dataset

Input:

Importing required libraries

from sklearn.datasets import load_breast_cancer as cancer

from sklearn.tree import DecisionTreeClassifier as DTC

from sklearn.model_selection import train_test_split as tss

import matplotlib.pyplot as plt

```
# Loading input data

value = cancer()


# Splitting input data into training and testing data

Data_trn, Data_tst, Target_trn, Target_tst = tss(value.data,
value.target, random_state=10)


accuracy_trn = []

accuracy_tst = []


limit = range(1, 11)

for i in limit:


    # Training the model

    dtc = DTC(criterion = 'entropy', min_samples_split = 50,
    max_features = 3, max_depth = 2)

    dtc.fit(Data_trn, Target_trn)
```

```python
    # Calculating accuracy of Training Data

accuracy_trn.append(dtc.score(Data_trn, Target_trn))

    # Calculating accuracy of Testing Data

accuracy_tst.append(dtc.score(Data_tst, Target_tst))


# Plotting accuracy of training and testing data

plt.plot(limit, accuracy_trn, label = "Accuracy of Training
Data")

plt.plot(limit, accuracy_tst, label = "Accuracy of Testing Data")

plt.xlabel("Value")

plt.ylabel("Accuracy")

plt.legend()
```

Output:

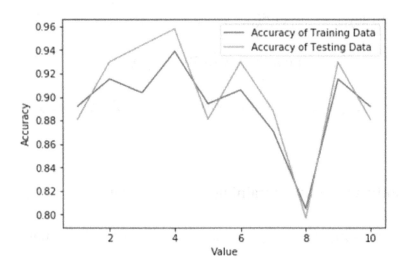

Accuracies accuracy of training and testing of Breast cancer dataset using DTC with 3 features

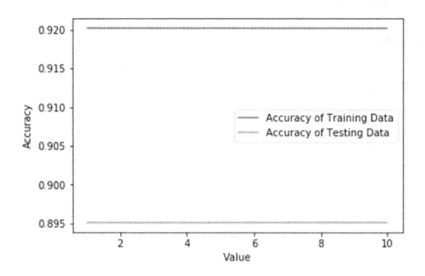

Accuracies of training and testing of Breast cancer dataset using DTC with 30 features

If you change the value of max_features (representing maximum features) from 3 to 30, the accuracy of DT algorithm will increase. Accuracy is increased with increase in number of features because the dataset contains 30 features. When the algorithm uses all features, the algorithm classifies effectively and hence accuracy is increased. While the accuracy of the DT algorithm increases with the increase in numbers and features, complexity and simulation time will increase as well.

dtc = DTC(criterion = 'entropy', min_samples_split = 50, max_features = 3, max_depth = 2)

Change parameters of DTC to check the results. You can see the effects of changing maximum features. If you try to change the value of features to more than 30, what will be the result?

You will be encountered with an error. Do not be alarmed as it can easily be explained. We have just surpassed the maximum value of features, which is why the program is unable to compute and hence returns an error.

Applying Decision Tree on Iris dataset

Input:

Importing required libraries

from sklearn.datasets import load_iris as iris

from sklearn.tree import DecisionTreeClassifier as DTC

from sklearn.model_selection import train_test_split as tss

import matplotlib.pyplot as plt

Loading input data

value = iris()

Data = value.data

Target = value.target

Splitting input data into training and testing data

Data_trn, Data_tst, Target_trn, Target_tst = tss(value.data, value.target, random_state=10)

```python
# Printing size of training and testing data

print(Data_trn.shape)

print(Data_tst.shape)


accuracy_trn = []

accuracy_tst = []


limit = range(1, 11)

for i in limit:

        # Training the model

    dtc = DTC(criterion = 'entropy', min_samples_split = 50,
    max_features = 3, max_depth = 2)

        dtc.fit(Data_trn, Target_trn)

        # Calculating accuracy of Training Data

    accuracy_trn.append(dtc.score(Data_trn, Target_trn))

        # Calculating accuracy of Testing Data

    accuracy_tst.append(dtc.score(Data_tst, Target_tst))

# Plotting accuracy of training and testing data
```

```
plt.plot(limit, accuracy_trn, label = "Accuracy of Training
Data")

plt.hold

plt.plot(limit, accuracy_tst, label = "Accuracy of Testing Data")

plt.xlabel("Value")

plt.ylabel("Accuracy")

plt.legend()


# Plotting prediction

plt.figure(2)

plt.plot(Data_trn[Target_trn == 0,0], Data_trn[Target_trn ==
0,1], 'rs', label = value.target_names[0])

plt.hold

plt.plot(Data_trn[Target_trn == 1,0], Data_trn[Target_trn ==
1,1], 'g.', label = value.target_names[1])

plt.legend()

plt.xlabel(value.feature_names[0])

plt.ylabel(value.feature_names[1])
```

Output:

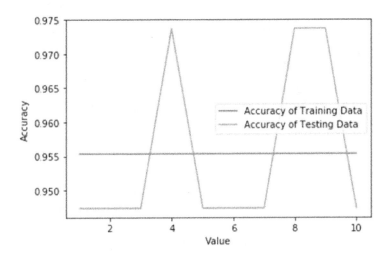

Accuracies of training and testing of iris dataset using DT with 3 features

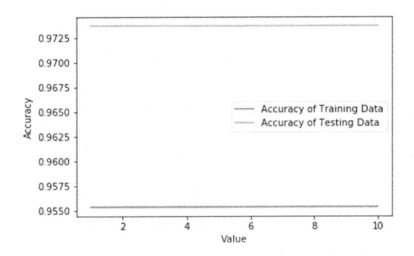

Accuracies of training and testing of iris dataset using DT with 4 features

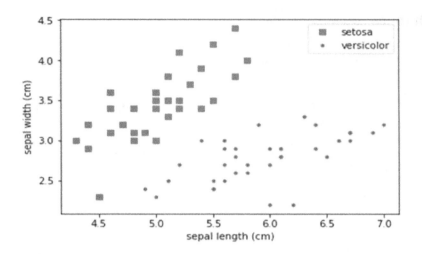

Predictions of iris dataset using DT with 3 features

By changing the value of max_features representing maximum features from three to four, you can observe that the accuracy of DT algorithm increases. As dataset contains four features and when algorithm uses all features, the algorithm classifies effectively and hence accuracy is increased and simulation time as well. Prediction achieved using four features instead of three is visually same, hence its plot is not shown.

dtc = DTC(criterion = 'entropy', min_samples_split = 50, max_features = 3, max_depth = 2)

Try changing the value to more than four. What results do you believe you will obtain? Again, do not worry should you encounter an error. This is to familiarize yourself with such situations and understanding the maximum values of such components. It is not necessary that these maximum values are predefined as we will look further in detail in future chapters.

Support Vector Machine

Support vector machines (SVM) are another example of machine learning, which is also used for both classification and regression processes. As it is used for supervised machine learning, labeled training data is given to a model. That model then assigns new values to these datasets. It works by creating categories separated by clear gap. The data belongs to a class, which is near to the line representing specific classes. This process proceeds until each dataset gets assigned.

Applying support vector classification on Breast cancer dataset

Input:

Importing required libraries

from sklearn.svm import SVC

from sklearn.datasets import load_breast_cancer as cancer

from sklearn.model_selection import train_test_split as tss

import matplotlib.pyplot as plt

```
# Loading input data

value = cancer()


# Splitting input data into training and testing data

Data_trn, Data_tst, Target_trn, Target_tst = tss(value.data,
value.target, random_state=10)


accuracy_trn = []

accuracy_tst = []


limit = range(1, 11)

for i in limit:

        # Training the model

        svc = SVC(C = 1.0, gamma = 'auto', kernel = 'rbf')

    svc.fit(Data_trn,Target_trn)

        # Calculating accuracy of Training Data

        accuracy_trn.append(svc.score(Data_trn, Target_trn))
```

Calculating accuracy of Testing Data

accuracy_tst.append(svc.score(Data_tst, Target_tst))

Plotting accuracy of training and testing data

plt.plot(limit, accuracy_trn, label="Accuracy of Training Data")

plt.plot(limit, accuracy_tst, label="Accuracy of Testing Data")

plt.xlabel("Neighbors")

plt.ylabel("Accuracy")

plt.legend()

Output:

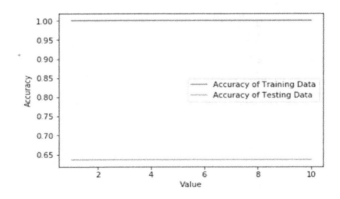

Accuracies of training and testing of Breast cancer dataset
using SVC with rbf kernel

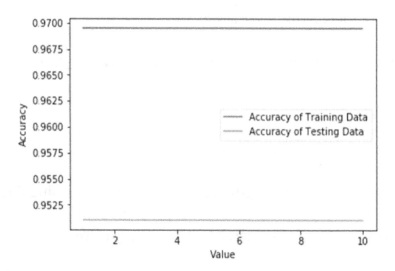

Accuracies of training and testing of Breast cancer dataset using SVC with linear kernel

By changing the kernel from 'rbf' to linear, it leads to better accuracy. The accuracy is increased because the problem is linear. The rbf can also work fine but in cases where problem is nonlinear.

svc = SVC(C = 1.0, gamma = 'auto', kernel = 'rbf')

Applying support vector classification on Iris dataset

Input:

```
# Importing required libraries

from sklearn.svm import SVC

from sklearn.datasets import load_iris as iris

from sklearn.model_selection import train_test_split as tss

import matplotlib.pyplot as plt

# Loading input data

value = iris()


# Splitting input data into training and testing data

Data_trn, Data_tst, Target_trn, Target_tst = tss(value.data,
value.target, random_state=10)

accuracy_trn = []

accuracy_tst = []


limit = range(1, 11)
```

```
for i in limit:

        # Training the model

        svc = SVC(C = 1.0, gamma = 'auto', kernel = 'rbf')

        svc.fit(Data_trn, Target_trn)

        # Calculating accuracy of Training Data

    accuracy_trn.append(svc.score(Data_trn, Target_trn))

        # Calculating accuracy of Testing Data

    accuracy_tst.append(svc.score(Data_tst, Target_tst))


# Plotting accuracy of training and testing data

plt.plot(limit, accuracy_trn, label = "Accuracy of Training
Data")

plt.plot(limit, accuracy_tst, label = "Accuracy of Testing Data")

plt.xlabel("Value")

plt.ylabel("Accuracy")

plt.legend()
```

```python
# Plotting prediction

plt.figure(2)

plt.plot(Data_trn[Target_trn == 0,0], Data_trn[Target_trn ==
0,1], 'rs', label = value.target_names[0])

plt.hold

plt.plot(Data_trn[Target_trn == 1,0], Data_trn[Target_trn ==
1,1], 'g.', label = value.target_names[1])

plt.legend()

plt.xlabel(value.feature_names[0])

plt.ylabel(value.feature_names[1])
```

Output:

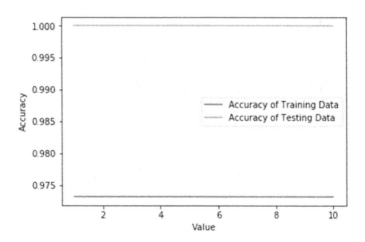

Accuracies of training and testing of iris dataset using SVC with rbf kernel

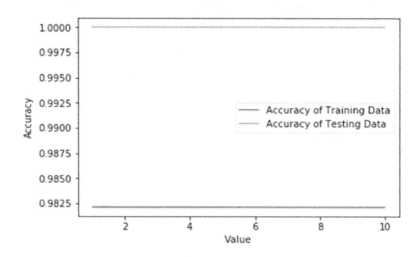

Accuracies of training and testing of iris dataset using SVC with linear kernel

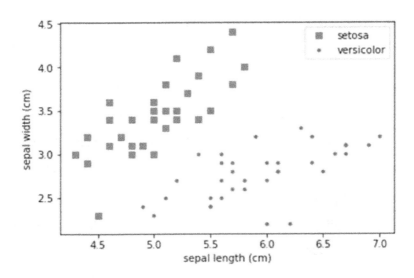

Predictions of iris dataset using SVC with rbf kernel

Again you can observe that by the change in the value of kernel from RBF to linear, the accuracy of the SVC algorithm increases. Accuracy is increased because problem is linear. The RBF can also work fine, but generally it is used in other cases where the problem is nonlinear. Predictions achieved using linear kernel instead of rbf kernel are visually the same and hold very minor details, not enough to be mapped or displayed, hence its plot is not shown.

svc = SVC(C = 1.0, gamma = 'auto', kernel = 'rbf')

Naive Bayes Classification

Naive Bayes classification method is another example of machine learning, which is used for classification process. This works by calculating probabilities of each dataset and assigns them new values depending on the value of their probabilities. This process continues until each dataset is assigned. Like previous methods, Naive Bayes will also be applied on both Iris and Breast cancer datasets for classification and then performances will be evaluated. Remember, you can use your preferred datasets instead of the ones shown in the book. The aim here is to provide you with a visual data representation of how accuracy varies and how we can use various methods on the same datasets to bring out unique results, based on the situation.

Applying naive Bayes classification on Breast cancer dataset

Input:

Importing required libraries

from sklearn.naive_bayes import GaussianNB as NB

from sklearn.datasets import load_breast_cancer as cancer

from sklearn.model_selection import train_test_split as tss

```python
import matplotlib.pyplot as plt


# Loading input data

value = cancer()


# Splitting input data into training and testing data

Data_trn, Data_tst, Target_trn, Target_tst = tss(value.data,
value.target, random_state=10)


accuracy_trn = []

accuracy_tst = []

limit = range(1, 11)

for i in limit:

        # Training the model

        nb = NB()

        nb.fit(Data_trn, Target_trn)

        # Calculating accuracy of Training Data
```

```
    accuracy_trn.append(nb.score(Data_trn, Target_trn))

        # Calculating accuracy of Testing Data

    accuracy_tst.append(nb.score(Data_tst, Target_tst))



# Plotting accuracy of training and testing data

plt.plot(limit, accuracy_trn, label = "Accuracy of Training
Data")

plt.plot(limit, accuracy_tst, label = "Accuracy of Testing Data")

plt.xlabel("Value")

plt.ylabel("Accuracy")

plt.legend()
```

Output:

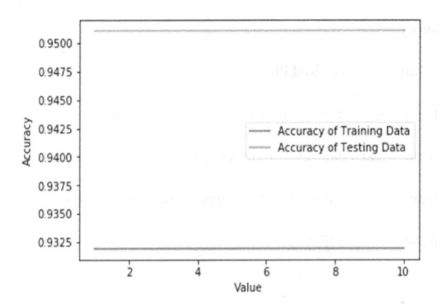

Accuracies of training and testing of Breast cancer dataset using NB

Naive Bayes method is applied with default settings of parameters. You can play with command below by passing various arguments:

nb = NB()

Applying naive Bayes classification on Iris dataset

Input:

Importing required libraries

from sklearn.naive_bayes import GaussianNB as NB

from sklearn.datasets import load_iris as iris

from sklearn.model_selection import train_test_split as tss

import matplotlib.pyplot as plt

Loading input data

value = iris()

Splitting input data into training and testing data

Data_trn, Data_tst, Target_trn, Target_tst = tss(value.data, value.target, random_state=10)

accuracy_trn = []

accuracy_tst = []

limit = range(1, 11)

```python
for i in limit:

        # Training the model

        nb = NB()

        nb.fit(Data_trn, Target_trn)

        # Calculating accuracy of Training Data

    accuracy_trn.append(nb.score(Data_trn, Target_trn))

        # Calculating accuracy of Testing Data

    accuracy_tst.append(nb.score(Data_tst, Target_tst))


# Plotting accuracy of training and testing data

plt.plot(limit, accuracy_trn, label = "Accuracy of Training
Data")

plt.plot(limit, accuracy_tst, label = "Accuracy of Testing Data")

plt.xlabel("Value")

plt.ylabel("Accuracy")

plt.legend()

# Plotting prediction

plt.figure(2)
```

```
plt.plot(Data_trn[Target_trn == 0,0], Data_trn[Target_trn ==
0,1], 'rs', label = value.target_names[0])
```

```
plt.hold
```

```
plt.plot(Data_trn[Target_trn == 1,0], Data_trn[Target_trn ==
1,1], 'g.', label = value.target_names[1])
```

```
plt.legend()
```

```
plt.xlabel(value.feature_names[0])
```

```
plt.ylabel(value.feature_names[1])
```

Output:

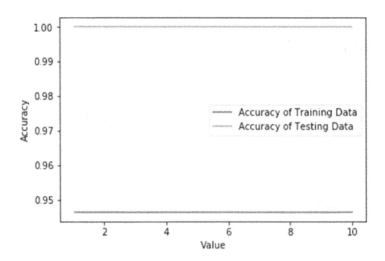

Accuracies of training and testing of Iris dataset using NB

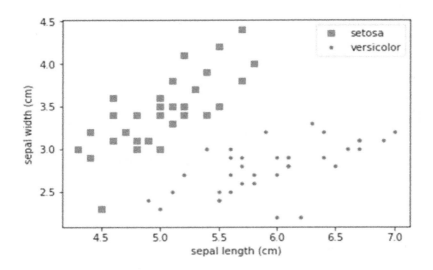

Predictions of iris dataset using NB

Logistic Regression

The logistic regression method is used for classification process as well for machine learning. Although its name suggests that this method may work better for the regression process, but it actually works just for classification process.

This method belongs to the linear classification. It can also be known as binary classification as it assigns zeros and ones to dataset in order to perform the process of classification. This method also works by calculating probabilities of each dataset and then assigns them new values depending on the value of their probabilities. Logistic Regression method will also be applied on both Iris and Breast cancer datasets for classification and then performances will be analyzed.

Applying logistic regression on Breast cancer dataset

Input:

```
# Importing required libraries

from sklearn.linear_model import LogisticRegression as LR

from sklearn.datasets import load_breast_cancer as cancer

from sklearn.model_selection import train_test_split as tss

import matplotlib.pyplot as plt


# Loading input data

value = cancer()


# Splitting input data into training and testing data

Data_trn, Data_tst, Target_trn, Target_tst = tss(value.data,
value.target, random_state=10)


accuracy_trn = []

accuracy_tst = []
```

```python
limit = range(1, 11)

for i in limit:


        # Training the model

        lr = LR(tol = 0.01, C = 1.0, max_iter = 100, n_jobs = 1)

        lr.fit(Data_trn, Target_trn)

        # Calculating accuracy of Training Data

        accuracy_trn.append(lr.score(Data_trn, Target_trn))

        # Calculating accuracy of Testing Data

    accuracy_tst.append(lr.score(Data_tst, Target_tst))


# Plotting accuracy of training and testing data

plt.plot(limit, accuracy_trn, label = "Accuracy of Training
Data")

plt.plot(limit, accuracy_tst, label = "Accuracy of Testing Data")

plt.xlabel("Value")

plt.ylabel("Accuracy")
```

plt.legend()

Output:

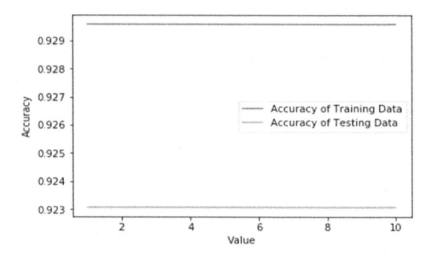

Accuracies of training and testing of Breast cancer dataset using LR with tolerance of 0.01

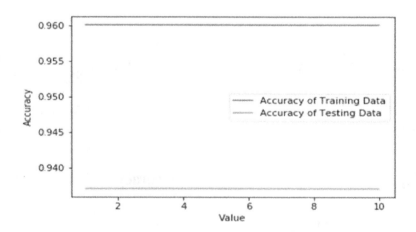

Accuracies of training and testing of Breast cancer dataset using LR with tolerance of 0.0001

By changing the value of tolerance from 0.01 to 0.0001 through the command shown below, the accuracy of LR algorithm is increased. Accuracy is increased as less tolerance is accepted. With decreasing tolerance, quality output is achieved.

lr = LR(tol = 0.01, C = 1.0, max_iter = 100, n_jobs = 1)

Experiment with the parameters and check how the results vary. You can try and change the value of max_iter as well. However, can the accuracy increase if we reduce the tolerance? That's something for you to check by manipulating the values.

Remember, experiments have lead to great discoveries, we are just trying to gain a bit of an understanding here. Through trial and error, we will soon be able to understand how most of these methods work and how the data output would be like when we change certain values.

Applying logistic regression on Iris dataset

Input:

Importing required libraries

from sklearn.linear_model import LogisticRegression as LR

from sklearn.datasets import load_iris as iris

```python
from sklearn.model_selection import train_test_split as tss

import matplotlib.pyplot as plt


# Loading input data

value = iris()


# Splitting input data into training and testing data

Data_trn, Data_tst, Target_trn, Target_tst = tss(value.data,
value.target, random_state=10)


accuracy_trn = []

accuracy_tst = []

limit = range(1, 11)

for i in limit:

        # Training the model

        lr = LR(tol = 0.01, C = 10.0, max_iter = 100, n_jobs = 1)

    lr.fit(Data_trn, Target_trn)
```

```python
# Calculating accuracy of Training Data

accuracy_trn.append(lr.score(Data_trn, Target_trn))

# Calculating accuracy of Testing Data

accuracy_tst.append(lr.score(Data_tst, Target_tst))


# Plotting accuracy of training and testing data

plt.plot(limit, accuracy_trn, label = "Accuracy of Training
Data")

plt.plot(limit, accuracy_tst, label = "Accuracy of Testing Data")

plt.xlabel("Value")

plt.ylabel("Accuracy")

plt.legend()


# Plotting prediction

plt.figure(2)

plt.plot(Data_trn[Target_trn == 0,0], Data_trn[Target_trn ==
0,1], 'rs', label = value.target_names[0])

plt.hold
```

plt.plot(Data_trn[Target_trn == 1,0], Data_trn[Target_trn == 1,1], 'g.', label = value.target_names[1])

plt.legend()

plt.xlabel(value.feature_names[0])

plt.ylabel(value.feature_names[1])

Output:

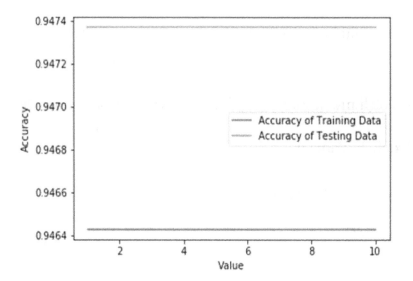

Accuracies of training and testing of Iris dataset using LR with C of 1

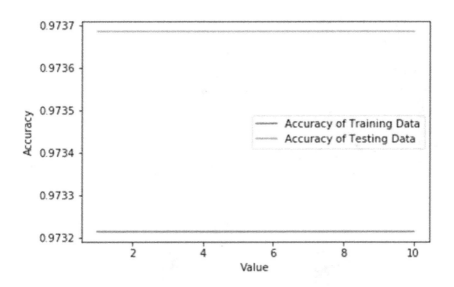

Accuracies of training and testing of Iris dataset using LR with C of 10

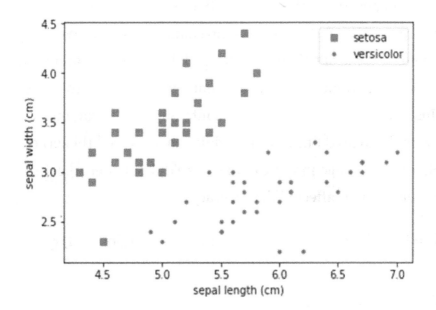

Predictions of iris dataset using LR using LR with C of 1

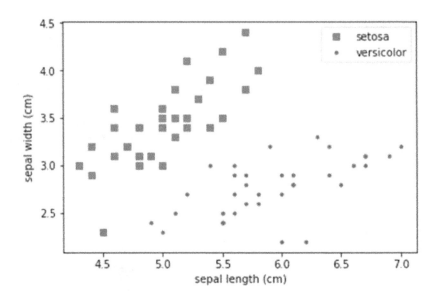

Predictions of iris dataset using LR with value of C of 10

You can observe in this example that by a change in the value of tolerance from 0.01 to 0.0001, no change appeared. We then changed value of C from 1 to 10 which increased the accuracy. Different parameters work differently for different problems. Just like we saw when we looked into Support vector, one example favored linear kernel while other favored rbf kernel. Similarly, change in value of tolerance did not affect the accuracy but C affected the accuracy.

lr = LR(tol = 0.01, C = 1.0, max_iter = 100, n_jobs = 1)

Neural Network

Neural network (NN) is another method of machine learning. It has been used often as a preferred method in machine learning problems. It uses multiple methods, which are modeled much similar to human brain to check patterns for predictions. We will apply NN for classification processes in this chapter. We will apply NN classification to Breast cancer and Iris datasets to validate its working capacity and accuracy.

Applying Neural network on Breast cancer dataset

Input:

```
# Importing required libraries

from keras.models import Sequential as NN

from keras.layers import Dense

from sklearn.datasets import load_breast_cancer as cancer

from sklearn.model_selection import train_test_split as tss

import matplotlib.pyplot as plt

import numpy as np
```

```python
# Loading input data

value = cancer()


# Splitting input data into training and testing data

Data_trn, Data_tst, Target_trn, Target_tst = tss(value.data,
value.target, random_state=10)

accuracy_trn = []

accuracy_tst = []


limit = range(1, 11)

for i in limit:


        # Training the model

        nn = NN()


        nn.add(Dense(1, activation = 'relu'))

        # compile the keras model
```

```
        nn.compile(loss = 'binary_crossentropy', optimizer =
'adam', metrics = ['accuracy'])

        # fit keras model on dataset

        nn.fit(Data_trn, Target_trn, epochs = 150, batch_size =
10)

        # Calculating accuracy of Training Data

    accuracy_trn.append(nn.evaluate(Data_trn, Target_trn))

        # Calculating accuracy of Testing Data

    accuracy_tst.append(nn.evaluate(Data_tst, Target_tst))


A = np.array([accuracy_trn])

B = np.array([accuracy_tst])


AA = A[0, :, 1]

BB = B[0, :, 1]


# Plotting accuracy of training and testing data

plt.plot(limit, AA, label = "Accuracy of Training Data")
```

plt.plot(limit, BB, label = "Accuracy of Testing Data")

plt.xlabel("Value")

plt.ylabel("Accuracy")

plt.legend()

Output:

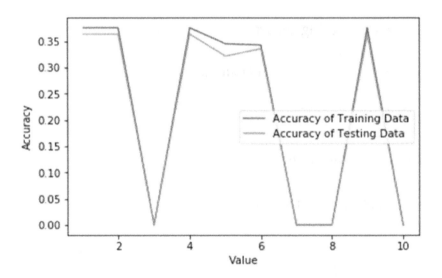

Accuracies of training and testing of Breast cancer dataset using NN with relu activation

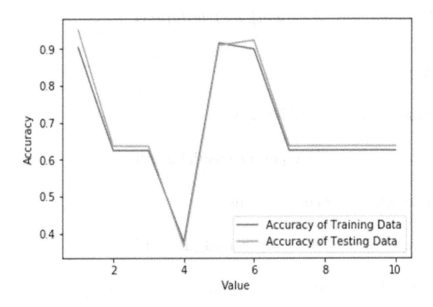

Accuracies of training and testing of Breast cancer dataset using NN with sigmoid activation

Change in the value of activation from 'relu' to 'sigmoid' in the command mentioned below, you can observe the increase in accuracy of NN algorithm.

nn.add(Dense(1, activation = 'relu'))

You can shuffle the activation to check the performance of the NN algorithm as well.

Applying Neural network on Iris dataset

Input:

```
# Importing required libraries

from keras.models import Sequential as NN

from keras.layers import Dense

from sklearn.datasets import load_iris as iris

from sklearn.model_selection import train_test_split as tss

import matplotlib.pyplot as plt

import numpy as np


# Loading input data

value = iris()


# Splitting input data into training and testing data

Data_trn, Data_tst, Target_trn, Target_tst = tss(value.data,
value.target, random_state=10)
```

```python
accuracy_trn = []

accuracy_tst = []


limit = range(1, 11)

for i in limit:

        # Training the model

        nn = NN()

        nn.add(Dense(1, activation = 'relu'))

        # compile the keras model

        nn.compile(loss = 'binary_crossentropy', optimizer =
'adam', metrics = ['accuracy'])

        # fit keras model on dataset

        nn.fit(Data_trn, Target_trn, epochs = 150, batch_size =
10)

        # Calculating accuracy of Training Data

    accuracy_trn.append(nn.evaluate(Data_trn, Target_trn))

        # Calculating accuracy of Testing Data

    accuracy_tst.append(nn.evaluate(Data_tst, Target_tst))
```

```python
A = np.array([accuracy_trn])

B = np.array([accuracy_tst])

AA = A[0, :, 1]

BB = B[0, :, 1]


# Plotting accuracy of training and testing data

plt.plot(limit, AA, label = "Accuracy of Training Data")

plt.plot(limit, BB, label = "Accuracy of Testing Data")

plt.xlabel("Value")

plt.ylabel("Accuracy")

plt.legend()


# Plotting prediction

plt.figure(2)

plt.plot(Data_trn[Target_trn == 0,0], Data_trn[Target_trn == 0,1], 'rs', label = value.target_names[0])

plt.hold
```

plt.plot(Data_trn[Target_trn == 1,0], Data_trn[Target_trn == 1,1], 'g.', label = value.target_names[1])

plt.legend()

plt.xlabel(value.feature_names[0])

plt.ylabel(value.feature_names[1])

Output:

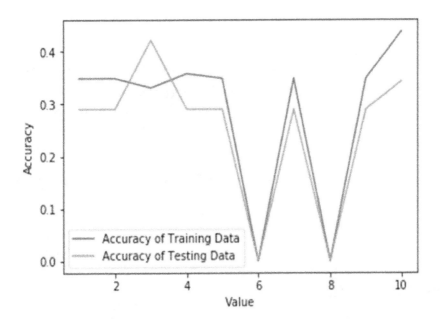

Accuracies of training and testing of Iris dataset using NN with relu activation

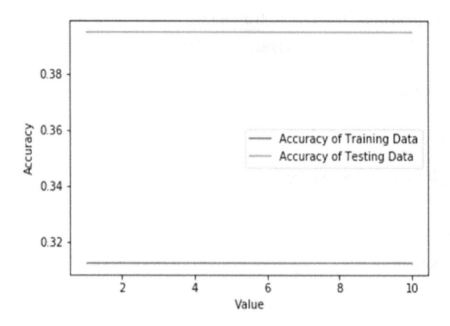

Accuracies of training and testing of Iris dataset using NN
with sigmoid activation

By changing the value further, you can observe the increase in accuracy of NN algorithm.

nn.add(Dense(1, activation = 'relu'))

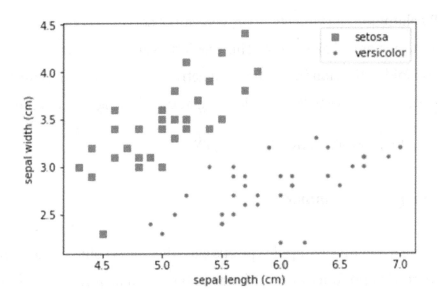

Predictions of iris dataset using NN with relu activation

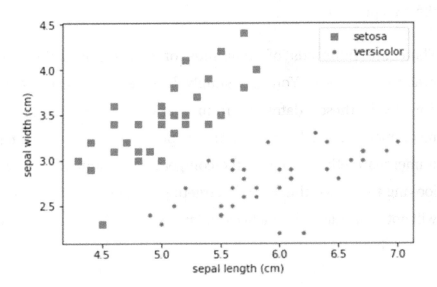

Predictions of iris dataset using NN with sigmoid activation

By changing the value further, you can observe the increase in accuracy of NN algorithm. The prediction achieved through sigmoid activation instead of relu activation is exactly the same, which is why we will not be looking at the plotting of the same.

```
nn.add(Dense(1, activation = 'relu'))
```

Things to remember:

We learned how we apply various classifications using numerous methods and functions. Each one of them has its unique use and application. Their accuracy in mapping and plotting varies, which is why it is ideal to get yourself familiarized with these through practice.

There are hundreds of thousands of datasets available for practice purposes. You can simply browse the internet and download these datasets from various websites. It is recommended that you continue practicing and learning numerous methods to gain the competitive advantage you are looking for. Since this book is targeting advanced learning, we will not continue with practices and move toward our next aspect of learning.

Chapter 3: Supervised Machine Learning for Continuous Class Label

Understanding the Concept of Regression

We already have discussed in the previous chapter that the term Supervised learning originated from the term supervision. Supervised learning takes data as inputs, and it also knows its corresponding outputs as well, and when different inputs are provided to that system, it can predict its output using that trained model.

We also discussed in the previous chapter that supervised machine learning comprises of two types: classification and regression. We discussed classification earlier in detail, which is used to predict discrete label, which means that it provides discrete output of specific input for training.

In this chapter, we will discuss the regression method that is used to predict continuous label which means that provides continuous output of specific input for training.

You can distinguish between two categories of supervised machine learning, classification and regression, by checking whether your output, given by prediction, contains any continuity or not. If the data contains continuity, then it is an example of regression and if it contains discrete output then it can safely be deduced as an example of classification. If you may recall, we already have discussed an example an individual's annual income when we initially touched upon regression.

We can have multiple applications of regression. We can have both sets of data either discrete or continuous. We need to understand both the schemes of machine learning in order to apply these methods in practical problems.

Regression Models

We have discussed the classification versions of KNN, Decision tree, SVM, Naive Bayes, logistic regression and Neural Network in the previous chapter. We applied those classification methods on Iris and Breast cancer datasets. Some of them contained features of regression as well.

There are many regression models that will be used in this chapter to predict continuous labels. We will discuss regression using KNN, Decision tree, SVM, Random forest, linear regression and Neural Network. We will apply these regression methods on Boston and Diabetes datasets; these are pre-defined datasets, available within the Scikit-Learn.

While performing the process of regression, we need to keep the factors of overfitting and underfitting in consideration. We need to know if our training datasets or models will work just on the training, test data and/or with new test data. We also should keep an eye out to know if we need to completely change the model to work for other test data.

K-Nearest Neighbors Regression

As we discussed in the previous chapter, KNN is the simplest machine learning algorithm that is used for both classification and regression processes. We used this method for classification process in the previous chapter, and this time, we will use it for the application of regression process.

The working procedure will remain the same for KNN for regression. This means, as before, it will take k nearest neighbors to calculate a new data point for any given data. If we keep value of k as one, it will be simplest version of KNN regression, which will take only one nearest neighbor as reference to calculate new data point for an input data. It will work exactly the same for calculating new data points for all the given data. We will apply the KNN-based regression to Boston and Diabetes datasets to analyze the accuracy. The value of K can also be varied to observe changes in the prediction.

Applying KNN regression on Boston dataset

Input:

Importing required libraries

from sklearn.neighbors import KNeighborsRegressor as KNN

from sklearn.datasets import load_boston as boston

from sklearn.model_selection import train_test_split as tss

import matplotlib.pyplot as plt

import pandas as pd

Loading input data

value = boston()

df = pd.DataFrame(value.data, columns = value.feature_names)

df["MEDV"] = value.target

X = df.drop("MEDV",1)   # Feature Matrix

Y = df["MEDV"]   # Target Vector

Splitting input data into training and testing data

```
Data_trn, Data_tst, Target_trn, Target_tst = tss(X, Y,
random_state = 10)
```

```
# Printing size of training and testing data

print(Data_trn.shape)

print(Data_tst.shape)
```

Output:

(379, 13)

(127, 13)

Input:

```
accuracy_trn = []

accuracy_tst = []


limit = range(1, 11)

for i in limit:
```

```python
# Training the model

knn = KNN(n_neighbors = 1)

knn.fit(Data_trn, Target_trn)

# Calculating accuracy of Training Data

accuracy_trn.append(knn.score(Data_trn, Target_trn))

# Calculating accuracy of Testing Data

accuracy_tst.append(knn.score(Data_tst, Target_tst))


# Plotting accuracy of training and testing data

plt.plot(limit, accuracy_trn, label = "Accuracy of Training Data")

plt.plot(limit, accuracy_tst, label = "Accuracy of Testing Data")

plt.xlabel("Value")

plt.ylabel("Accuracy")

plt.legend()
```

Output:

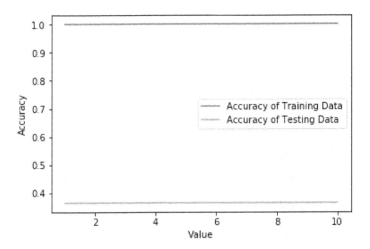

Accuracies of training and testing on Boston dataset using KNN with 2 neighbors

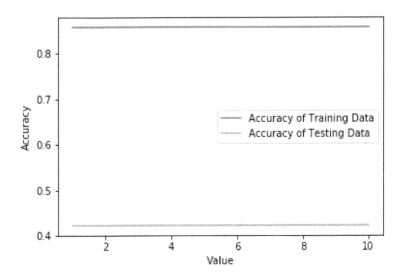

Accuracies of training and testing on Boston dataset using KNN with 3 neighbors

As before, if we change the value of n_neighbors while predicting its output from 1 to 2, we can observe the increase in accuracy of the KNN algorithm. Increasing the value of the nearest neighbors, the accuracy of KNN algorithm also increases. However, by increasing too many nearest neighbors, the complexity and simulation time increases as well.

Similarly, by using a much bigger value of number for neighbors, it can lead to lesser classes. You can further change value of k to check the change in accuracy of the prediction. Try to use different values for the code and analyze the performance of KNN algorithm. You can also apply this code to another dataset as well.

knn = KNN(n_neighbors = 2)

Applying KNN regression on Diabetes dataset

Input:

Importing required libraries

from sklearn.neighbors import KNeighborsRegressor as KNN

from sklearn.datasets import load_diabetes as diabetes

from sklearn.model_selection import train_test_split as tss

import matplotlib.pyplot as plt

```python
import pandas as pd


# Loading input data

value = diabetes()

df = pd.DataFrame(value.data, columns =
value.feature_names)

df["MEDV"] = value.target

X = df.drop("MEDV",1)   # Feature Matrix

Y = df["MEDV"]      # Target Vector


# Splitting input data into training and testing data

Data_trn, Data_tst, Target_trn, Target_tst = tss(X, Y,
random_state = 10)


# Printing size of training and testing data

print(Data_trn.shape)

print(Data_tst.shape)
```

Output:

(331, 10)

(111, 10)

Input:

accuracy_trn = []

accuracy_tst = []

limit = range(1, 11)

for i in limit:

```
# Training the model
knn = KNN(n_neighbors = 2)
knn.fit(Data_trn, Target_trn)
# Calculating accuracy of Training Data
accuracy_trn.append(knn.score(Data_trn, Target_trn))
# Calculating accuracy of Testing Data
accuracy_tst.append(knn.score(Data_tst, Target_tst))
```

Plotting accuracy of training and testing data

plt.plot(limit, accuracy_trn, label = "Accuracy of Training Data")

plt.plot(limit, accuracy_tst, label = "Accuracy of Testing Data")

plt.xlabel("Value")

plt.ylabel("Accuracy")

plt.legend()

Output:

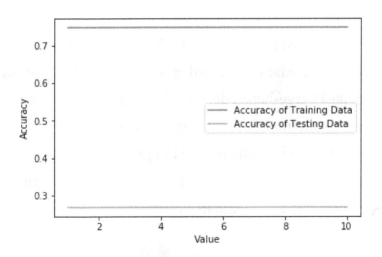

Accuracies of training and testing on Diabetes dataset using KNN with 2 neighbors

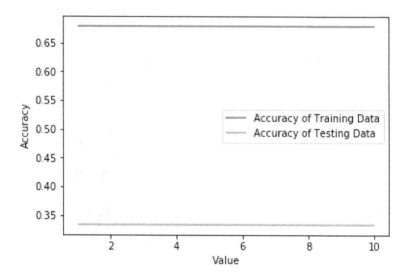

Accuracies of training and testing on Diabetes dataset using KNN with 3 neighbors

Decision Tree Regression

We have discussed in the previous chapter about usage of Decision Tree method for classification process. We discussed that it makes a tree-based decision in classifying the data sets. We used this method for classification process previously but in this chapter, we will apply regression process using Decision tree regression. We will apply Decision tree to Boston and Diabetes datasets to validate its accuracy.

Applying Decision Tree regression on Boston dataset

Input:

Importing required libraries

from sklearn.tree import DecisionTreeRegressor as DTR

from sklearn.datasets import load_boston as boston

from sklearn.model_selection import train_test_split as tss

import matplotlib.pyplot as plt

import pandas as pd

Loading input data

value = boston()

df = pd.DataFrame(value.data, columns = value.feature_names)

df["MEDV"] = value.target

X = df.drop("MEDV",1)   # Feature Matrix

Y = df["MEDV"]   # Target Vector

```python
# Splitting input data into training and testing data

Data_trn, Data_tst, Target_trn, Target_tst = tss(X, Y,
random_state = 10)


accuracy_trn = []

accuracy_tst = []

limit = range(1, 11)

for i in limit:

        # Training the model

        dtr = DTR(min_samples_split = 50, max_features = 3,
max_depth = 2)

        dtr.fit(Data_trn, Target_trn)

        # Calculating accuracy of Training Data

    accuracy_trn.append(dtr.score(Data_trn, Target_trn))

        # Calculating accuracy of Testing Data

    accuracy_tst.append(dtr.score(Data_tst, Target_tst))
```

Plotting accuracy of training and testing data

plt.plot(limit, accuracy_trn, label = "Accuracy of Training Data")

plt.plot(limit, accuracy_tst, label = "Accuracy of Testing Data")

plt.xlabel("Value")

plt.ylabel("Accuracy")

plt.legend()

Output:

Accuracies accuracy of training and testing of Boston dataset using DTR with 3 features

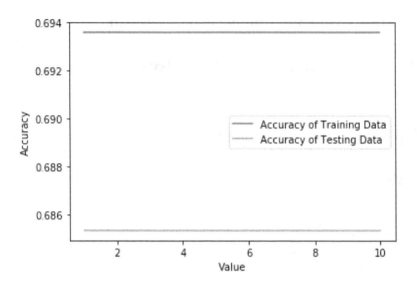

Accuracies of training and testing of Boston cancer dataset using DTR with 13 features

If we change the value of max_features, which represents the maximum features of the algorithm, from 3 to 13 in the below-mentioned command, we can observe that the accuracy of DT algorithm is greatly increased. Accuracy is increased with increase in the number of features because the dataset actually contains all 13 features and when algorithm uses all features, the algorithm is classified effectively and hence the accuracy is spot on.

As with the increase in the value of features, accuracy of DT algorithm increases, along with the complexity and the simulation time. Owing to the nature of this output, we need to strike a healthy balance between accuracy and simulation time.

dtr = DTR(min_samples_split = 50, max_features = 3, max_depth = 2)

You can again change value of max_features to check the change in accuracy of the prediction. Go ahead and change the values to analyze the performance of DTR algorithm. You should apply this code to other dataset as well to see how it performs with them.

Applying Decision Tree regression on Diabetes dataset

Input:

Importing required libraries

from sklearn.tree import DecisionTreeRegressor as DTR

from sklearn.datasets import load_diabetes as diabetes

from sklearn.model_selection import train_test_split as tss

import matplotlib.pyplot as plt

import pandas as pd

Loading input data

value = diabetes()

df = pd.DataFrame(value.data, columns =

```python
value.feature_names)

df["MEDV"] = value.target

X = df.drop("MEDV",1)   # Feature Matrix

Y = df["MEDV"]       # Target Vector


# Splitting input data into training and testing data

Data_trn, Data_tst, Target_trn, Target_tst = tss(X, Y,
random_state = 10)


accuracy_trn = []

accuracy_tst = []


limit = range(1, 11)

for i in limit:

        # Training the model

        dtr = DTR(min_samples_split = 50, max_features = 3,
max_depth = 2)

        dtr.fit(Data_trn, Target_trn)
```

```python
# Calculating accuracy of Training Data

accuracy_trn.append(dtr.score(Data_trn, Target_trn))

# Calculating accuracy of Testing Data

accuracy_tst.append(dtr.score(Data_tst, Target_tst))


# Plotting accuracy of training and testing data

plt.plot(limit, accuracy_trn, label = "Accuracy of Training Data")

plt.plot(limit, accuracy_tst, label = "Accuracy of Testing Data")

plt.xlabel("Value")

plt.ylabel("Accuracy")

plt.legend()
```

Output:

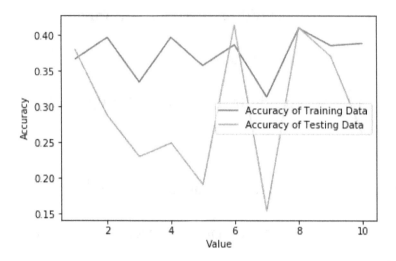

Accuracies of training and testing of iris dataset using DTR with 3 features

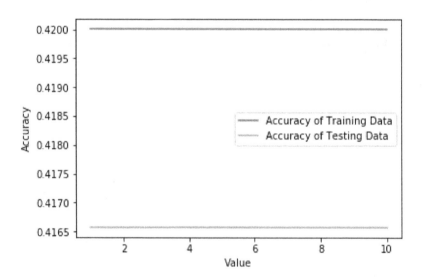

Accuracies of training and testing of iris dataset using DTR with 10 features

Support Vector Regression

We have discussed Support vector machines in a previous chapter. We have discussed its classification method in that chapter, and we will apply SVM for regression process in this chapter. We will apply SVM to Boston and Diabetes datasets to validate its accuracy. As it belongs to supervised machine learning, labeled training data are given to that model, and that model assigns new values to these datasets. It creates categories separated by clear gap. The data belongs to class which is near to that line representing specific class. This process proceeds until each data set gets assigned.

Applying support vector regression on Boston dataset

Input:

Importing required libraries

from sklearn.svm import SVR

from sklearn.datasets import load_boston as boston

from sklearn.model_selection import train_test_split as tss

import matplotlib.pyplot as plt

import pandas as pd

```python
# Loading input data

value = boston()

df = pd.DataFrame(value.data, columns =
value.feature_names)

df["MEDV"] = value.target

X = df.drop("MEDV",1)   # Feature Matrix

Y = df["MEDV"]      # Target Vector


# Splitting input data into training and testing data

Data_trn, Data_tst, Target_trn, Target_tst = tss(X, Y,
random_state = 10)


accuracy_trn = []

accuracy_tst = []


limit = range(1, 11)

for i in limit:

        # Training the model
```

```python
svr = SVR(C = 1.0, gamma = 'auto', kernel = 'rbf')

svr.fit(Data_trn, Target_trn)

# Calculating accuracy of Training Data

accuracy_trn.append(svr.score(Data_trn, Target_trn))

# Calculating accuracy of Testing Data

accuracy_tst.append(svr.score(Data_tst, Target_tst))


# Plotting accuracy of training and testing data

plt.plot(limit, accuracy_trn, label = "Accuracy of Training
Data")

plt.plot(limit, accuracy_tst, label = "Accuracy of Testing Data")

plt.xlabel("Value")

plt.ylabel("Accuracy")

plt.legend()
```

Output:

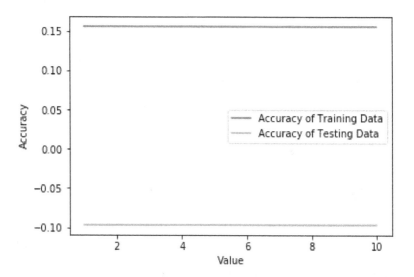

Accuracies of training and testing of Boston dataset using SVR with rbf kernel

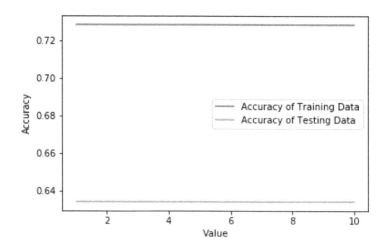

Accuracies of training and testing of Boston dataset using SVR with linear kernel

svr = SVR(C = 1.0, gamma = 'auto', kernel = 'rbf')

You can change the kernel value above to linear, as the above case is linear in nature, to improve the accuracy. Remember, had this been a nonlinear version, we would have preferred the 'RBF' instead.

Changing values of kernel is a great way to check the change in accuracy of the prediction. You can change the value of C as well. In many cases, C plays a vital role; however, will it play its role in this algorithm? Try it out yourself and see what happens when you change the value of C to anything else than 1.0.

While you practice using these methods and codes, try to change the value of gamma as well. Sometimes, you may need to fine tune your adjustments and values in order to bring out the best results and accuracy possible. If you are presented with an error, you would immediately know that the program is unable to compute using the given values and hence you can find out about their minimum and maximum values as well.

Applying support vector regression on Diabetes dataset

Input:

```python
# Importing required libraries

from sklearn.svm import SVR

from sklearn.datasets import load_diabetes as diabetes

from sklearn.model_selection import train_test_split as tss

import matplotlib.pyplot as plt

import pandas as pd


# Loading input data

value = diabetes()

df = pd.DataFrame(value.data, columns = value.feature_names)

df["MEDV"] = value.target

X = df.drop("MEDV",1)   # Feature Matrix

Y = df["MEDV"]      # Target Vector
```

```python
# Splitting input data into training and testing data

Data_trn, Data_tst, Target_trn, Target_tst = tss(X, Y,
random_state = 10)


accuracy_trn = []

accuracy_tst = []


limit = range(1, 11)

for i in limit:

        # Training the model

        svr = SVR(C = 1000.0, gamma = 'auto', kernel = 'rbf')

        svr.fit(Data_trn, Target_trn)

        # Calculating accuracy of Training Data

    accuracy_trn.append(svr.score(Data_trn, Target_trn))

        # Calculating accuracy of Testing Data

    accuracy_tst.append(svr.score(Data_tst, Target_tst))
```

Plotting accuracy of training and testing data

plt.plot(limit, accuracy_trn, label = "Accuracy of Training Data")

plt.plot(limit, accuracy_tst, label = "Accuracy of Testing Data")

plt.xlabel("Value")

plt.ylabel("Accuracy")

plt.legend()

Output:

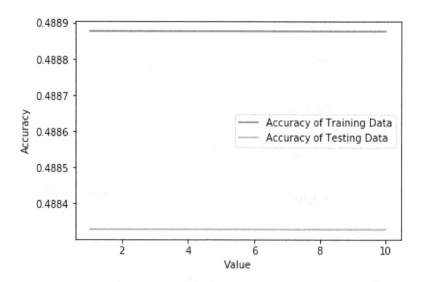

Accuracies of training and testing of Diabetes dataset using SVR with rbf kernel

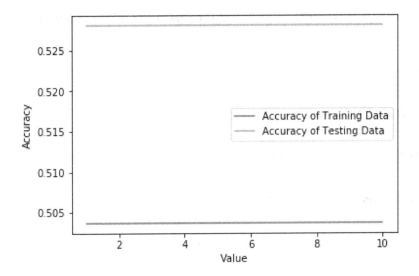

Accuracies of training and testing of Diabetes dataset using SVR with linear kernel

Random Forest Regression

Random forest method is another example of machine learning that is mainly used for regression process. This also work same as decision tree to some extent as it calculates probabilities of each data set and assign them new values depending on the value of their probabilities. It is used to take mode of classes or mean of trees in order to predict new value of data. This process proceeds until each data set get assigned. We will apply Random forest regression to Boston and Diabetes datasets to analyze its working and accuracy.

Applying Random Forest Regression on Boston dataset

Input:

```
# Importing required libraries

from sklearn.ensemble import RandomForestRegressor as RFR

from sklearn.datasets import load_boston as boston

from sklearn.model_selection import train_test_split as tss

import matplotlib.pyplot as plt

import pandas as pd


# Loading input data

value = diabetes()

df = pd.DataFrame(value.data, columns = value.feature_names)

df["MEDV"] = value.target

X = df.drop("MEDV",1)   # Feature Matrix

Y = df["MEDV"]      # Target Vector
```

```python
# Splitting input data into training and testing data

Data_trn, Data_tst, Target_trn, Target_tst = tss(X, Y,
random_state = 10)


accuracy_trn = []

accuracy_tst = []


limit = range(1, 11)

for i in limit:

        # Training the model

        rfr = RFR(n_estimators = 10, random_state = 0)

        rfr.fit(Data_trn, Target_trn)

        # Calculating accuracy of Training Data

        accuracy_trn.append(rfr.score(Data_trn, Target_trn))

        # Calculating accuracy of Testing Data

    accuracy_tst.append(rfr.score(Data_tst, Target_tst))

# Plotting accuracy of training and testing data
```

```
plt.plot(limit, accuracy_trn, label = "Accuracy of Training
Data")

plt.plot(limit, accuracy_tst, label = "Accuracy of Testing Data")

plt.xlabel("Value")

plt.ylabel("Accuracy")

plt.legend()
```

Output:

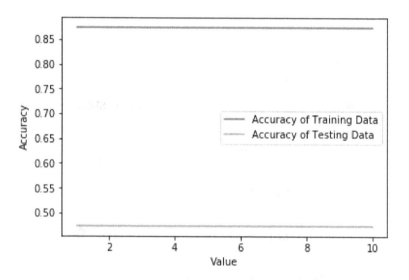

Accuracies of training and testing of Boston dataset using RFR with n_estimators of 10

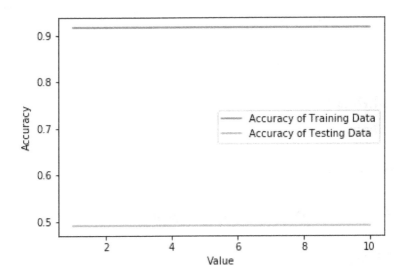

Accuracies of training and testing of Boston dataset using RFR with n_estimators of 100

Applying Random Forest Regression on Diabetes dataset

Input:

Importing required libraries

from sklearn.ensemble import RandomForestRegressor as RFR

from sklearn.datasets import load_diabetes as diabetes

from sklearn.model_selection import train_test_split as tss

import matplotlib.pyplot as plt

import pandas as pd

```python
# Loading input data

value = diabetes()

df = pd.DataFrame(value.data, columns =
value.feature_names)

df["MEDV"] = value.target

X = df.drop("MEDV",1)   # Feature Matrix

Y = df["MEDV"]       # Target Vector


# Splitting input data into training and testing data

Data_trn, Data_tst, Target_trn, Target_tst = tss(X, Y,
random_state = 10)


accuracy_trn = []

accuracy_tst = []


limit = range(1, 11)

for i in limit:

        # Training the model
```

```
rfr = RFR(n_estimators = 10, random_state = 0)

rfr.fit(Data_trn, Target_trn)

# Calculating accuracy of Training Data

accuracy_trn.append(rfr.score(Data_trn, Target_trn))

    # Calculating accuracy of Testing Data

accuracy_tst.append(rfr.score(Data_tst, Target_tst))


# Plotting accuracy of training and testing data

plt.plot(limit, accuracy_trn, label = "Accuracy of Training
Data")

plt.plot(limit, accuracy_tst, label = "Accuracy of Testing Data")

plt.xlabel("Value")

plt.ylabel("Accuracy")

plt.legend()
```

Output:

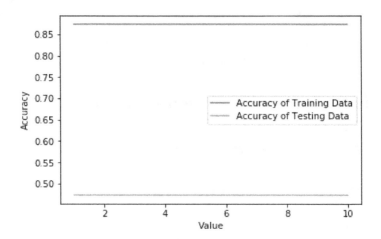

Accuracies of training and testing of Diabetes dataset using RFR with n_estimators of 10

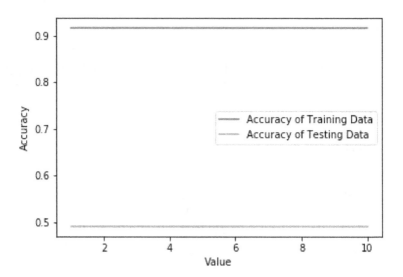

Accuracies of training and testing of Diabetes dataset using RFR with n_estimators of 100

In both the examples here and above, one parameter is playing a vital part. Changing that will alter the rate of accuracy. This is represented as:

rfr = RFR(n_estimators = 10, random_state = 0)

You can try to modify the value of n_estimators, which denotes the number of estimators. You can vary the numeric value from 10 to 100 and see how the accuracy is affected. Alternatively, you can also try to change the value of the random_state variable to anything other than zero.

Linear Regression

Linear regression method is another basic method of machine learning that is just used for regression process. This method belongs to linear classification. As its name suggests, once the model is trained, it uses linear functions to predict the output value of given data. These models are also known as linear models. This method is being used much as compare to other predictive methods. The reason behind its success is that the models that rely linearly on unknown parameters can fit better than those models who rely nonlinearly on unknown parameters. This process proceeds until each data set get assigned. We will apply linear regression to Boston and Diabetes datasets to validate its working and accuracy.

Applying linear regression on Boston dataset

Input:

```
# Importing required libraries

from sklearn.linear_model import LinearRegression as LR

from sklearn.datasets import load_boston as boston

from sklearn.model_selection import train_test_split as tss

import matplotlib.pyplot as plt

import pandas as pd


# Loading input data

value = boston()

df = pd.DataFrame(value.data, columns = value.feature_names)

df["MEDV"] = value.target

X = df.drop("MEDV",1)   # Feature Matrix

Y = df["MEDV"]     # Target Vector
```

```python
# Splitting input data into training and testing data

Data_trn, Data_tst, Target_trn, Target_tst = tss(X, Y,
random_state = 10)


accuracy_trn = []

accuracy_tst = []


limit = range(1, 11)

for i in limit:

        # Training the model

        rf = LR(n_jobs = 1)

        rf.fit(Data_trn, Target_trn)

        # Calculating accuracy of Training Data

        accuracy_trn.append(rf.score(Data_trn, Target_trn))

        # Calculating accuracy of Testing Data

    accuracy_tst.append(rf.score(Data_tst, Target_tst))
```

Plotting accuracy of training and testing data

```
plt.plot(limit, accuracy_trn, label = "Accuracy of Training
Data")

plt.plot(limit, accuracy_tst, label = "Accuracy of Testing Data")

plt.xlabel("Value")

plt.ylabel("Accuracy")

plt.legend()
```

Output:

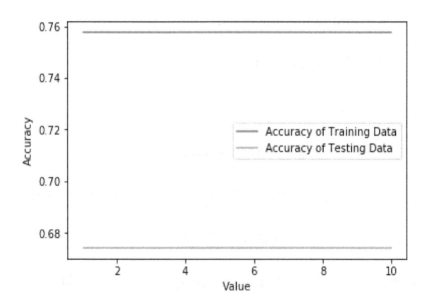

Accuracies of training and testing of Boston dataset using LR

Have a look at the command highlighted below. We can see that once again a single parameter plays a vital role to run this method.

rf = LR(n_jobs = 1)

Change value of n_jobs and check the result. Try to find out how large can you set its value.

Applying linear regression on Diabetes dataset

Input:

Importing required libraries

from sklearn.linear_model import LinearRegression as LR

from sklearn.datasets import load_diabetes as diabetes

from sklearn.model_selection import train_test_split as tss

import matplotlib.pyplot as plt

import pandas as pd

Loading input data

value = diabetes()

df = pd.DataFrame(value.data, columns =

```
value.feature_names)

df["MEDV"] = value.target

X = df.drop("MEDV",1)   # Feature Matrix

Y = df["MEDV"]      # Target Vector


# Splitting input data into training and testing data

Data_trn, Data_tst, Target_trn, Target_tst = tss(X, Y,
random_state = 10)


accuracy_trn = []

accuracy_tst = []


limit = range(1, 11)

for i in limit:

        # Training the model

        rf = LR(n_jobs = 1)

        rf.fit(Data_trn, Target_trn)
```

```python
    # Calculating accuracy of Training Data

accuracy_trn.append(rf.score(Data_trn, Target_trn))

    # Calculating accuracy of Testing Data

accuracy_tst.append(rf.score(Data_tst, Target_tst))


# Plotting accuracy of training and testing data

plt.plot(limit, accuracy_trn, label = "Accuracy of Training
Data")

plt.plot(limit, accuracy_tst, label = "Accuracy of Testing Data")

plt.xlabel("Value")

plt.ylabel("Accuracy")

plt.legend()
```

Output:

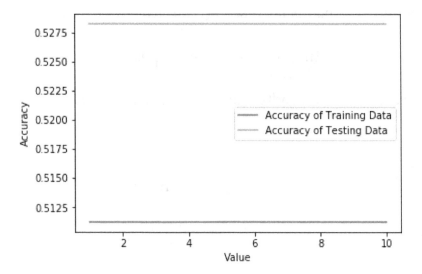

Accuracies of training and testing of Diabetes dataset using
LR

By applying various methods to the same datasets, we can see how the variations occur and how much accuracy we can obtain. While the charts may seemingly appear the same, the finer details are being changed to either provide a greater accuracy or otherwise.

Neural Network Regression

We have discussed the application of NN in terms of classification in a previous chapter. Now, we shall apply the NN for regression process. We will apply NN regression to Boston and Diabetes datasets to validate its working and accuracy.

Applying neural network regression on Boston dataset

Input:

Importing required libraries

from sklearn.neural_network import MLPRegressor as MLPR

from sklearn.datasets import load_boston as boston

from sklearn.model_selection import train_test_split as tss

import matplotlib.pyplot as plt

import pandas as pd

Loading input data

value = boston()

```python
df = pd.DataFrame(value.data, columns = value.feature_names)

df["MEDV"] = value.target

X = df.drop("MEDV",1)   # Feature Matrix

Y = df["MEDV"]        # Target Vector


# Splitting input data into training and testing data

Data_trn,  Data_tst,  Target_trn,  Target_tst  =  tss(X,  Y,
random_state = 10)


accuracy_trn = []

accuracy_tst = []


limit = range(1, 11)

for i in limit:

        # Training the model

        mlpr  =  MLPR(activation  =  'tanh',max_iter  =  1000,
random_state = 0)

        mlpr.fit(Data_trn, Target_trn)
```

```python
        # Calculating accuracy of Training Data

    accuracy_trn.append(mlpr.score(Data_trn, Target_trn))

        # Calculating accuracy of Testing Data

    accuracy_tst.append(mlpr.score(Data_tst, Target_tst))


# Plotting accuracy of training and testing data

plt.plot(limit, accuracy_trn, label = "Accuracy of Training Data")

plt.plot(limit, accuracy_tst, label = "Accuracy of Testing Data")

plt.xlabel("Value")

plt.ylabel("Accuracy")

plt.legend()
```

Output:

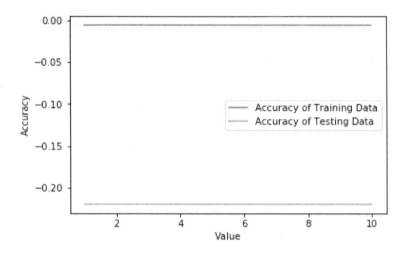

Accuracies of training and testing of Boston dataset using NN
with max_iters of 100

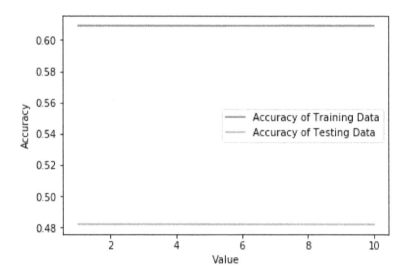

Accuracies of training and testing of Boston dataset using NN
with max_iters of 1000

We can observe that NN algorithm is using 'tanh' as activation. If we change the value of max_iter, which represents the maximum iterations from 100 to 1000, we can observe the increase in accuracy of the NN algorithm. It is obvious that accuracy of any algorithm increases with the increase in number of iterations. It takes quite a bit of processing to perform any task. It might consume more time, but it will come up with a better accuracy.

```
mlpr = MLPR(activation = 'tanh',max_iter = 1000,
random_state = 0)
```

Applying neural network regression on Diabetes dataset

Input:

```
# Importing required libraries

from sklearn.neural_network import MLPRegressor as MLPR

from sklearn.datasets import load_diabetes as diabetes

from sklearn.model_selection import train_test_split as tss

import matplotlib.pyplot as plt

import pandas as pd
```

```
# Loading input data

value = diabetes()

df = pd.DataFrame(value.data, columns =
value.feature_names)

df["MEDV"] = value.target

X = df.drop("MEDV",1)   # Feature Matrix

Y = df["MEDV"]       # Target Vector

# Splitting input data into training and testing data

Data_trn, Data_tst, Target_trn, Target_tst = tss(X, Y,
random_state = 10)


accuracy_trn = []

accuracy_tst = []


limit = range(1, 11)

for i in limit:

        # Training the model

        mlpr = MLPR(activation = 'tanh',max_iter = 1000,
```

```
random_state = 0)

    mlpr.fit(Data_trn, Target_trn)

    # Calculating accuracy of Training Data

  accuracy_trn.append(mlpr.score(Data_trn, Target_trn))

    # Calculating accuracy of Testing Data

  accuracy_tst.append(mlpr.score(Data_tst, Target_tst))


# Plotting accuracy of training and testing data

plt.plot(limit, accuracy_trn, label = "Accuracy of Training
Data")

plt.plot(limit, accuracy_tst, label = "Accuracy of Testing Data")

plt.xlabel("Value")

plt.ylabel("Accuracy")

plt.legend()
```

Output:

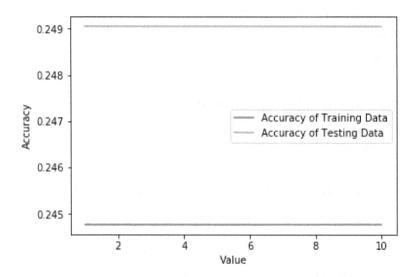

Accuracies of training and testing of Diabetes dataset using NN with max_iters of 1000

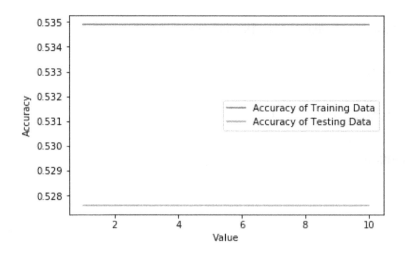

Accuracies of training and testing of Diabetes dataset using NN with max_iters of 10000

Once again, the NN algorithm is using tanh as activation. If we change the value of max_iter from 1000 to 10000, it will increase the accuracy of the NN algorithm. It is therefore understandable that accuracy of any algorithm increases with the increase in number of iterations.

In the previous chapter, we learned about discrete class labels and classification methods; however, this chapter introduced us to continuous class label classification methods. We went through a few examples and used Boston and Diabetes datasets to draw outputs from.

In the next chapter, we will be diving into the world of unsupervised learning to see just why it is slightly difficult to get a grasp on things. We will look into the concept of clustering and map out a few examples and codes to see how we can use unsupervised learning to bring out results that we require.

It is of the utmost importance that you continue practicing the codes to develop a firm understanding of the matter. Learning "Machine Learning" within a matter of days is not possible without ample practice, clarification of concepts and the usage of the right tools, libraries and understanding of Python as a programming language.

Chapter 4: Unsupervised Machine Learning

Earlier, at the start of the first chapter, we discussed how unsupervised learning is a method of machine learning that is used to gather information from the datasets. However, unlike supervised learning, it does not know the outputs to specific inputs, and when other inputs are given to it, it can just categorize outputs on the basis of some parameters such as Euclidean distance, etc. In short, unsupervised learning does not create datasets to be used for training the model for prediction of outputs.

Understanding the Concept of Clustering

Clustering can easily be defined as a method that partitions or divides the given data into sets of groups. These groups are called clusters. Each cluster contains data that is specific and contains items, components or data that matches. Think of two clusters named 'even' and 'odd,' One of these will contain numbers that are even, while the other would contain numbers that are odd.

There are two main types of unsupervised learning: transformation and clustering. The transformation method can relate with dimension reduction. It takes a high dimensional data, containing many samples of each features or many features, and converts it into low dimensional data. It removes less impactful samples or features.

In many cases, dimension reduction methods reduce to two dimensions. It is very important to apply dimension reduction methods as it can save processing time and avoid confusion, which is usually created when seeing high dimensional data. The dimension reduction methods provide a much-needed motivation to the programmer to dive deep into the data and visualize it better.

The other method of unsupervised learning is clustering. It is used to divide the data on the basis of similarities. If you want to deal with big data, you need it to be divided into multiple groups so that you can carry out efficient and effective analysis. For example, if you want to upload multiple photos to any social media site, you would like to add those photos in groups so that you can keep track of those pictures easily, if and when required. One way would be to add pictures of a similar person in one group. Although the sites don't know about you personally and don't know which picture represents whom, but the site still wants us to divide those pictures into groups as it is a sensible way of managing data.

Challenges in Unsupervised Learning

Unsupervised learning does not contain any information of label, which means we do not know the right output for the corresponding input. The model cannot come to a conclusion whether it went well or not. In such a case, algorithms will divide data on the basis of similarity of some of their features, and while doing so, it does not ensure the output of our choices.

For example, the model can group pictures in a way that one group will contain picture with various people in it, which does not necessarily fulfill the requirement of one who wants to have a group on the basis of individuals (each group containing pictures of a specific person).

Unsupervised learning can be used in cases where a programmer just wishes to understand the data instead of using it for any automation solution. Similarly, unsupervised learning can be used as a *preprocessing* step for supervised learning. In some cases, it might help to get better accuracy from supervised learning, and it can get less memory data and might be able to save time as well.

Preprocessing and Scaling

Many classification and regression methods have been discussed in previous chapters. We have observed that some of these methods require some work as their accuracies are not up to the mark. Some unsupervised-based preprocessing steps and scaling is performed before applying supervised methods.

Types of Preprocessing

There are different types of preprocessing. StandardScalar is one of the libraries used for preprocessing. It makes sure that each feature of dataset has a mean of zero and variance of one. It is used to keep all features to the same level. Although it does not have any specific minimum or maximum values for features, but it still works fine as it contains features of maintaining required mean and variance.

RobustScaler is another library that is used for preprocessing. It is also used to keep all features to the same level. It uses median and quartiles instead of mean and variance. Due to using different parameters, it ignores the data points which are far away from others. These data points are often known as outliers, which create complications for other scaling methods. Hence, RobustScaler is better in use than StandardScalar.

Then we have the MinMaxScaler library, which is used for preprocessing. It is used to keep the data between 0 and 1 by shifting the data. That means that if the data is plotted, then the scale of the x-axis and y-axis will be between 0 and 1. It can also produce acceptable results.

Normalizer is the last library to be discussed for preprocessing. It scales data points in a way that keeps the distance between the feature vectors of unity. Every data point is scaled at a different value. It is normally used when direction does matter.

Effects of Preprocessing on Supervised Learning

Preprocessing plays a very important role, especially for methods that are sensitive to these scalers. As mentioned earlier, many preprocessing scales can be used. Below is an example of preprocessing using MinMaxScaler.

Input:

```
# Importing required libraries

from sklearn.svm import SVC

from sklearn.datasets import load_breast_cancer as cancer

from sklearn.model_selection import train_test_split as tss

import matplotlib.pyplot as plt

from sklearn.preprocessing import MinMaxScaler as MMS


# Loading input data

value = cancer()
```

```
# Splitting input data into training and testing data

Data_trn, Data_tst, Target_trn, Target_tst = tss(value.data,
value.target,

                                        random_state = 10)

accuracy_trn = []

accuracy_tst = []

Data_trn_scld = []

Data_tst_scld = []


mms = MMS()

mms.fit(Data_trn)


Data_trn_scld = mms.transform(Data_trn)

Data_tst_scld = mms.transform(Data_tst)


limit = range(1, 11)

for i in limit:
```

```python
# Training the model

svc = SVC(C = 1.0, gamma = 'auto', kernel = 'rbf')

svc.fit(Data_trn_scld, Target_trn)

# Calculating accuracy of Training Data

accuracy_trn.append(svc.score(Data_trn_scld, Target_trn))

# Calculating accuracy of Testing Data

accuracy_tst.append(svc.score(Data_tst_scld,
Target_tst))


# Plotting accuracy of training and testing data

plt.plot(limit, accuracy_trn, label = "Accuracy of Training Data")

plt.plot(limit, accuracy_tst, label = "Accuracy of Testing Data")

plt.xlabel("Value")

plt.ylabel("Accuracy")

plt.legend()
```

Output:

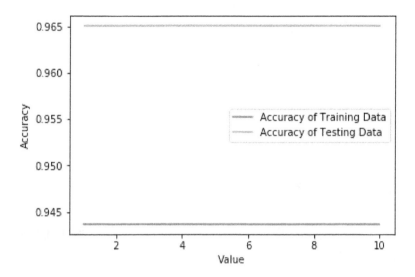

Accuracies of training and testing of Breast cancer dataset using SVC with MinMaxScaler

Let us look at an example of preprocessing using the StandardScaler.

Input:

Importing required libraries

from sklearn.svm import SVC

from sklearn.datasets import load_breast_cancer as cancer

from sklearn.model_selection import train_test_split as tss

import matplotlib.pyplot as plt

```python
from sklearn.preprocessing import StandardScaler as SS


# Loading input data

value = cancer()


# Splitting input data into training and testing data

Data_trn, Data_tst, Target_trn, Target_tst = tss(value.data,
value.target,

                                        random_state = 10)

accuracy_trn = []

accuracy_tst = []

Data_trn_scld = []

Data_tst_scld = []


ss = SS()

ss.fit(Data_trn)
```

```
Data_trn_scld = ss.transform(Data_trn)

Data_tst_scld = ss.transform(Data_tst)


limit = range(1, 11)

for i in limit:

        # Training the model

        svc = SVC(C = 1.0, gamma = 'auto', kernel = 'rbf')

        svc.fit(Data_trn_scld, Target_trn)

        # Calculating accuracy of Training Data

    accuracy_trn.append(svc.score(Data_trn_scld, Target_trn))

        # Calculating accuracy of Testing Data

    accuracy_tst.append(svc.score(Data_tst_scld, Target_tst))


# Plotting accuracy of training and testing data

plt.plot(limit, accuracy_trn, label = "Accuracy of Training
Data")

plt.plot(limit, accuracy_tst, label = "Accuracy of Testing Data")
```

plt.xlabel("Value")

plt.ylabel("Accuracy")

plt.legend()

Output:

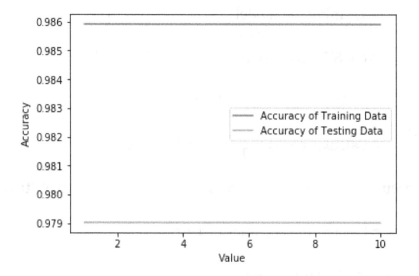

Accuracies of training and testing of Breast cancer dataset using SVC with StandardScaler

You can observe that SVM based classification provided an accuracy of around 0.64, but when we applied the MinMaxScaler based scaling and then applied classification using SVM, an accuracy of around 0.97 is achieved. Similarly, when we applied the StandardScaler based scaling and then applied classification using SVM, an accuracy of around 0.98

was achieved. Results can show that preprocessing is required, and MinMaxScaler and StandardScaler based preprocessing perform well.

Dimension Reduction

Many datasets contain high dimensions, which take long processing times. Along with processing problems, these datasets become difficult to visualize. Dimension reduction is required to reduce the dimensions of high dimensional datasets. It is also very important to retain maximum information even after reducing dimensions of the datasets. There are many methods that are used for dimension reduction.

Principal Component Analysis is famous for dimension reduction. It provides the principal components of the datasets. It removes the least impactful features and retains the highest impactful ones. This way, the datasets will not lose much information and will still be able to represent all the data.

Principal Component Analysis

Principal Component Analysis is a statistical method that works on orthogonal transformation to measure the correlation between variables. It finds out the principal components of datasets. An example of Dimension reduction using PCA is given below.

Applying Principal Component Analysis on Breast cancer dataset

Input [1]:

Importing required libraries

from sklearn.decomposition import PCA

from sklearn.datasets import load_breast_cancer as cancer

from sklearn.model_selection import train_test_split as tss

import matplotlib.pyplot as plt

from sklearn.preprocessing import StandardScaler as SS

Loading input data

value = cancer()

Splitting input data into training and testing data

Data_trn, Data_tst, Target_trn, Target_tst = tss(value.data, value.target, random_state = 10)

Data_trn_scld = []

Data_tst_scld = []

```python
ss = SS()

ss.fit(Data_trn)


Data_trn_scld = ss.transform(Data_trn)

Data_tst_scld = ss.transform(Data_tst)


# Training the model with Principal components of 2

pca = PCA(n_components = 2)

pca.fit(Data_trn_scld)

X_pca = pca.transform(Data_trn_scld)


print("Original Dimension:
{}".format(str(Data_trn_scld.shape)))

print("Reduced Dimension: {}".format(str(X_pca.shape)))
```

Output [1]:

Original Dimension: (426, 30)

Reduced Dimension: (426, 2)

Input [2]:

plotting First versus second principal component

plt.plot(X_pca[Target_trn == 0,0], X_pca[Target_trn == 0,1], 'rs', label = value.target_names[0])

plt.hold

plt.plot(X_pca[Target_trn == 1,0], X_pca[Target_trn == 1,1], 'g.', label = value.target_names[1])

plt.legend()

plt.xlabel("First principal component")

plt.ylabel("Second principal component")

Output [2]:

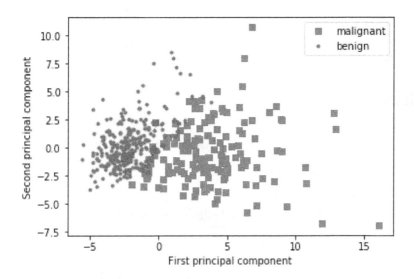

First Principal component versus Second Principal component of Breast cancer dataset using PCA and StandardScaler

Input [2]:

```
print("Dimension of PCA components:
{}".format(pca.components_.shape))
```

Output [2]:

Dimension of PCA components: (2, 30)

Input [3]:

```python
print("Components of PCA:\n{}".format(pca.components_))
```

Output [3]:

Components of PCA:

[[0.22497118 0.10209091 0.23305712 0.22669916
0.13095741 0.23777761

  0.26054451 0.26113228 0.11857964 0.04990416
0.20451814 0.01547142

  0.21189041 0.2032527 0.00835308 0.17314863
0.18095912 0.18353095

  0.03353539 0.10045326 0.23188534 0.09793079
0.24072506 0.22923198

  0.11457974 0.20876477 0.22872514 0.2501444
0.10389674 0.12133481]

 [-0.22383928 -0.06901511 -0.20453941 -0.22094646
0.20201801 0.16857578

  0.04865932 -0.02438319 0.19604069 0.37928075 -
0.09722973 0.0862208

  -0.07797413 -0.13996098 0.20813873 0.237834
0.17790854 0.12701146

0.18413975 0.28625985 -0.21230329 -0.06003402 -
0.1898874 -0.21147895

0.18822065 0.14823507 0.08302158 -0.00246167
0.13405653 0.28669719]]

Applying Principal Component Analysis on Digits dataset

Input [1]:

Importing required libraries

from sklearn.decomposition import PCA

from sklearn.datasets import load_digits as Value

import matplotlib.pyplot as plt

Plotting Digits Dataset

value = Value()

fig, axes = plt.subplots(2, 5, figsize=(10, 5),

subplot_kw={'xticks':(), 'yticks': ()})

for ax, img in zip(axes.ravel(), value.images):

    ax.imshow(img)

Training the model with Principal components of 2

pca = PCA(n_components = 2)

pca.fit(value.data)

PCA Transform

value_pca = pca.transform(value.data)

colors = ["#A83683", "#4E655E", "#853541", "#3A3120", "#535D8E",

"#476A2A", "#7851B8", "#BD3430", "#4A2D4E", "#875525"]

Output [1]:

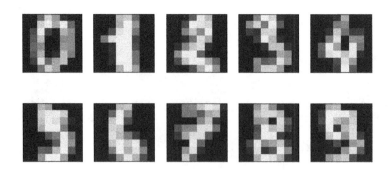

Digits dataset

Input [2]:

```python
# Plotting Principal components

plt.figure(figsize = (10, 10))

plt.xlim(value_pca[:, 0].min(), value_pca[:, 0].max())

plt.ylim(value_pca[:, 1].min(), value_pca[:, 1].max())


for i in range(len(value.data)):

    plt.text(value_pca[i, 0], value_pca[i, 1], str(value.target[i]), color =

        colors[value.target[i]], fontdict = {'weight': 'bold', 'size': 9})

plt.xlabel("First principal component")

plt.ylabel("Second principal component")
```

Output [2]:

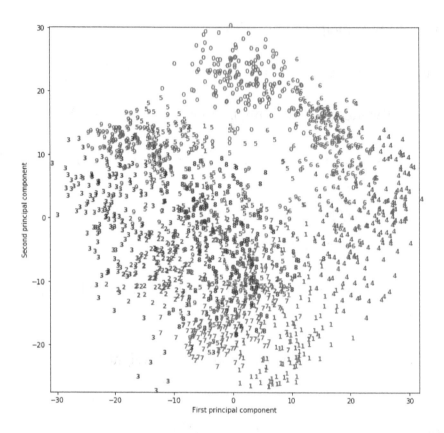

First Principal component versus Second Principal component
of Digits dataset using PCA

Manifold Learning with t-SNE

We have discussed PCA for dimension reduction and data
visualization. t-SNE is another method that is used to visualize
data. It provides a better visualization of data as compared to
PCA. An example of visualization of data using t-SNE method is
given below.

Applying t-SNE on Digits dataset

Input:

```
# Importing required libraries

from sklearn.manifold import TSNE

from sklearn.datasets import load_digits as Value

import matplotlib.pyplot as plt


value = Value()

tsne = TSNE(random_state = 42)


# TSNE Transform

value_tsne = tsne.fit_transform(value.data)

colors = ["#A83683", "#4E655E", "#853541", "#3A3120",
"#535D8E",

"#476A2A", "#7851B8", "#BD3430", "#4A2D4E", "#875525"]


# Plotting Feature components

plt.figure(figsize = (10, 10))
```

```
plt.xlim(value_tsne[:, 0].min(), value_tsne[:, 0].max() + 1)

plt.ylim(value_tsne[:, 1].min(), value_tsne[:, 1].max() + 1)

for i in range(len(value.data)):

    plt.text(value_tsne[i, 0], value_tsne[i, 1],
str(value.target[i]),color = colors[value.target[i]],fontdict =
{'weight': 'bold', 'size': 9})

plt.xlabel("First Feature of t-SNE")

plt.xlabel("Second Feature of t-SNE")
```

Output :

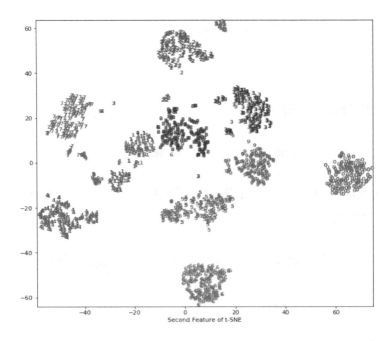

First Feature component versus Second Feature component of
Digits dataset using t-SNE

You can observe through the result that t-SNE method is far better than PCA in terms of visualization of data. It divided classes better than PCA method. There are other methods as well for visualization of data.

Clustering Models

We already know that clustering is used to divide the dataset into groups known as clusters. As it belongs to unsupervised machine learning, it deals without the knowledge of labels. There are many methods for clustering process. We will discuss K-Means clustering, Agglomerative clustering, and DBSCAN methods.

K-Means Clustering

K-means clustering is a commonly used method due to it being the simplest method of clustering. It finds the center of clusters that belong to certain regions of dataset. The user gives an input to the method by providing the required number of clusters, and by using that information, it starts with random centers of those number of clusters, takes the mean of these cluster centers with each data point, and then finds the updated cluster center. It keeps on doing this process in multiple iterations until no further change is detected. The result can be contradictory as method does not have the knowledge of labels, so it just makes the clusters by using specific techniques.

Applying K-Means Clustering on Blobs dataset

Input [1]:

```python
# Importing required libraries

from sklearn.datasets import make_blobs as blobs

from sklearn.cluster import KMeans

import matplotlib.pyplot as plt


# Reading input data

Data, Target = blobs(random_state = 1)

# Making clustering model

kmeans = KMeans(n_clusters = 3)

kmeans.fit(Data)

print("Clusters:\n{}".format(kmeans.labels_))
```

Output [1]:

Clusters:

[0 2 2 2 1 1 1 2 0 0 2 2 1 0 1 1 1 0 2 2 1 2 1 0 2 1 1 0 0 1 0 0 1 0 2 1
2

2 2 1 1 2 0 2 2 1 0 0 0 0 2 1 1 1 0 1 2 2 0 0 2 1 1 2 2 1 0 1 0 2 2 2 1
0

0 2 1 1 0 2 0 2 2 1 0 0 0 0 2 0 1 0 0 2 2 1 1 0 1 0]

Input [2]:

print("Predictions:\n{}".format(kmeans.predict(Data)))

Output [2]:

Predictions:

[0 2 2 2 1 1 1 2 0 0 2 2 1 0 1 1 1 0 2 2 1 2 1 0 2 1 1 0 0 1 0 0 1 0 2 1
2

2 2 1 1 2 0 2 2 1 0 0 0 0 2 1 1 1 0 1 2 2 0 0 2 1 1 2 2 1 0 1 0 2 2 2 1
0

0 2 1 1 0 2 0 2 2 1 0 0 0 0 2 0 1 0 0 2 2 1 1 0 1 0]

Input [3]:

plt.scatter(X[: , 0], X[: , 1], c = kmeans.labels_)

plt.legend()

plt.xlabel(kmeans.labels_[0])

plt.ylabel(kmeans.labels_[1])

plt.hold

plt.show

Output [3]:

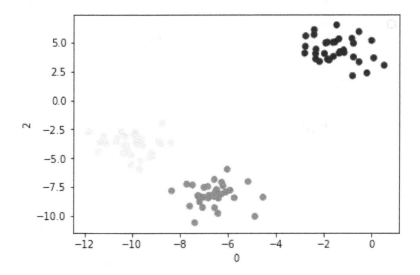

Prediction of Blobs Dataset using K-Means

Applying K-Means Clustering on Dense Blobs dataset

Input [1]:

Importing required libraries

from sklearn.datasets import make_blobs as blobs

from sklearn.cluster import KMeans

```python
import matplotlib.pyplot as plt

# Reading input data

Data, Target = blobs(n_samples = 200,cluster_std = [1.0, 2.5, 0.5],random_state = 170)

# Making clustering model

kmeans = KMeans(n_clusters = 3, random_state = 0)

kmeans.fit(Data)

print("Clusters:\n{}".format(kmeans.labels_))
```

Output [1]:

Clusters:

[1 2 2 0 0 1 2 0 1 0 2 1 1 0 1 2 0 0 1 0 1 0 0 1 0 0 0 0 2 1 2 0 1 1 0 1
2

 2 1 1 2 0 1 0 2 0 2 2 0 2 2 1 1 2 1 0 2 2 0 2 2 0 1 1 2 1 2 0 1 1 2 2 1
1

 2 2 0 2 1 2 2 0 1 1 0 0 0 1 0 2 0 0 0 0 2 0 0 0 2 2 1 1 2 0 1 1 2 1 1
2 2

 1 0 1 1 2 2 0 0 0 0 1 1 2 1 0 1 1 1 1 2 0 1 0 0 1 0 0 1 1 1 2 1 0 0 2 0 1

1 0 2 1 0 1 1 1 2 1 2 2 0 1 1 0 0 0 1 0 1 1 1 0 0 0 2 0 0 0 0 0 0 2 0 2
2

1 0 2 0 1 0 1 2 1 2 0 0 0 0 2]

Input [2]:

print("Predictions:\n{}".format(kmeans.predict(Data)))

Output [2]:

Predictions:

[1 2 2 0 0 1 2 0 1 0 2 1 1 0 1 2 0 0 1 0 1 0 0 1 0 0 0 0 2 1 2 0 1 1 0 1
2

2 1 1 2 0 1 0 2 0 2 2 0 2 2 1 1 2 1 0 2 2 0 2 2 0 1 1 2 1 2 0 1 1 2 2 1
1

2 2 0 2 1 2 2 0 1 1 0 0 0 1 0 2 0 0 0 0 2 0 0 0 2 2 1 1 2 0 1 1 2 1 1
2 2

1 0 1 1 2 2 0 0 0 0 1 1 2 1 0 1 1 1 2 0 1 0 0 1 0 0 1 1 1 2 1 0 0 2 0 1

1 0 2 1 0 1 1 1 2 1 2 2 0 1 1 0 0 0 1 0 1 1 1 0 0 0 2 0 0 0 0 0 0 2 0 2
2

1 0 2 0 1 0 1 2 1 2 0 0 0 0 2]

Input [3]:

plt.scatter(Data[: , 0], Data[: , 1], c = kmeans.labels_)

plt.xlabel(kmeans.labels_[0])

plt.ylabel(kmeans.labels_[1])

plt.hold

plt.show

Output [3]:

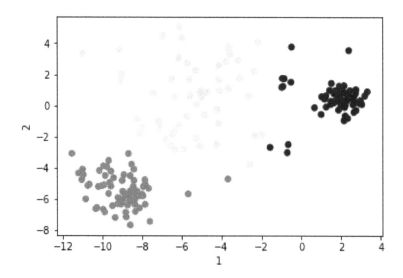

Prediction of Dense Blobs Dataset using K-Means

Applying K-Means Clustering on Stretched Blobs dataset

Input [1]:

```python
# Importing required libraries

from sklearn.datasets import make_blobs as blobs

from sklearn.cluster import KMeans

import matplotlib.pyplot as plt

import numpy as np


# Reading input data

Data, Target = blobs(random_state = 170, n_samples = 600)

rnd = np.random.RandomState(74)


# Data stretching through transformation

transformation = rnd.normal(size = (2, 2))

Data = np.dot(Data, transformation)


# Making clustering model
```

```
kmeans = KMeans(n_clusters = 3)

kmeans.fit(Data)


plt.scatter(Data[: , 0], Data[: , 1], c = kmeans.labels_)

plt.xlabel(kmeans.labels_[0])

plt.ylabel(kmeans.labels_[1])

plt.hold

plt.show
```

Output:

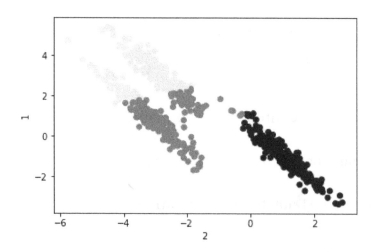

Prediction of Stretched Blobs Dataset using K-Means

You can observe that as long as we are making complex data, the performance of k-means method is decreasing. We are trying more complex data to further validate its performance.

Applying K-Means Clustering on Moons dataset

Input [1]:

Importing required libraries

from sklearn.datasets import make_moons as moons

from sklearn.cluster import KMeans

import matplotlib.pyplot as plt

Reading input data

Data, Target = moons(n_samples = 200, noise = 0.05, random_state = 0)

Making clustering model

kmeans = KMeans(n_clusters = 2)

kmeans.fit(Data)

```
plt.scatter(Data[: , 0], Data[: , 1], c = kmeans.labels_)

plt.xlabel(kmeans.labels_[0])

plt.ylabel(kmeans.labels_[1])

plt.hold

plt.show
```

Output:

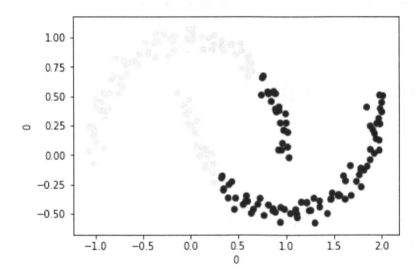

Prediction of Moons Dataset using K-Means

Here, we can evidently see that K-means was performing well on simple data, but when we moved to the Moons dataset, which is comparatively complex than Blobs dataset, K-means failed to make proper clusters. Both predicted classes contain members of other classes. We can analyze that k-Means does not work on complex datasets. For these problems, we need to look for other clustering methods.

Agglomerative Clustering

Agglomerative clustering is another method of clustering, which is somehow similar to the K-means clustering method as it also starts with random cluster. It then merges those clusters into similar clusters until no change occurs. We will apply Agglomerative clustering on blobs dataset to compare its performance with k-means.

Applying Agglomerative Clustering on Blobs dataset

Input:

Importing required libraries

from sklearn.datasets import make_blobs as blobs

from sklearn.cluster import AgglomerativeClustering as Agg

import matplotlib.pyplot as plt

Reading input data

Data, Target = blobs(random_state = 1)

Making clustering model

```
agg = Agg(n_clusters = 3)

agg.fit_predict(Data)


plt.scatter(Data[: , 0], Data[: , 1], c = agg.labels_)

plt.legend()

plt.xlabel(agg.labels_[0])

plt.ylabel(agg.labels_[1])

plt.hold

plt.show
```

Output:

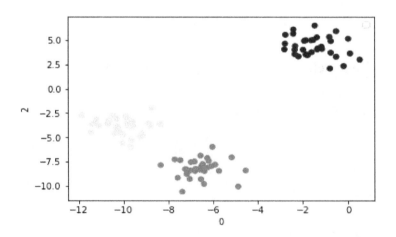

Prediction of Blobs Dataset using Agglomerative Clustering

You can observe that the performance of the Agglomerative clustering is much better than that of K-means clustering as it made clusters effectively. It has made clear clusters as compared to the ones K-means clustering came up with.

Applying Agglomerative Clustering on Moons dataset

Input:

Importing required libraries

from sklearn.datasets import make_moons as moons

from sklearn.cluster import AgglomerativeClustering as Agg

import matplotlib.pyplot as plt

Reading input data

Data, Target = moons(random_state = 1)

Making clustering model

agg = Agg(n_clusters = 3)

agg.fit_predict(Data)

```
plt.scatter(Data[:,0], Data[:,1], c = agg.labels_)

plt.legend()

plt.xlabel(agg.labels_[0])

plt.ylabel(agg.labels_[1])

plt.hold

plt.show
```

Output:

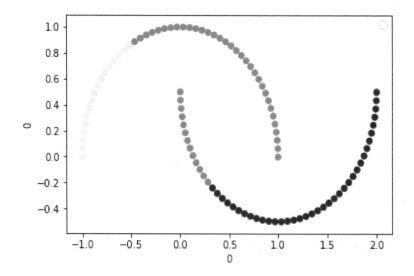

Prediction of Moons Dataset using Agglomerative Clustering

You can again observe that although the Agglomerative
clustering method could not perform perfectly in prediction of

the Moons dataset, its performance is still much better than K-means clustering.

DBSCAN

DBSCAN is yet another clustering method that is different from previous clustering methods we have looked upon so far. It works on points that are situated in the crowd region. Those crowd regions are also known as dense regions. It performs slower than Agglomerative clustering but gives better results than K-means clustering and Agglomerative clustering. Let us look at how this fares by applying the DBSCAN on moons dataset.

Applying DBSCAN Clustering on Blobs dataset

Input:

Importing required libraries

from sklearn.datasets import make_blobs as blobs

from sklearn.cluster import DBSCAN as DB

import matplotlib.pyplot as plt

Reading input data

```
Data, Target = blobs(random_state = 0, n_samples = 12)
```

```
# Making clustering model
```

```
db = DB()
```

```
dd = db.fit_predict(Data)
```

```
print("Cluster:\n{}".format(dd))
```

Output:

Cluster:

[-1 -1 -1 -1 -1 -1 -1 -1 -1 -1 -1 -1]

Applying DBSCAN Clustering on Moons dataset

Input [1]:

```
# Importing required libraries
```

```
from sklearn.datasets import make_moons as moons
```

```python
from sklearn.preprocessing import StandardScaler as SS

from sklearn.cluster import DBSCAN as DB

import matplotlib.pyplot as plt


# Reading input data

Data, Target = moons(n_samples = 200, noise = 0.05,
random_state = 0)

ss = SS()

ss.fit(Data)

Data_scaled = ss.transform(Data)


# Making clustering model

db = DB()

dd = db.fit_predict(Data_scaled)


print("Cluster:\n{}".format(dd))
```

Output [1]:

Cluster:

[0 1 1 0 1 1 0 1 0 1 0 1 1 1 0 0 0 1 0 0 1 1 0 1 0 1 1 1 1 0 0 0 1 1 0 1 1

0 0 1 1 0 0 1 1 0 0 0 1 1 0 1 1 0 1 0 0 1 0 0 1 0 1 0 1 0 0 1 0 0 1 0 1
1

1 0 1 0 0 1 1 0 1 1 1 0 0 0 1 1 0 0 1 0 1 1 1 1 0 1 1 1 0 0 0 1 0 0 1 0 0

0 0 0 0 1 0 1 1 0 0 0 1 0 1 0 0 1 1 1 0 0 0 1 1 1 1 0 1 0 1 1 0 0 0 0 1
1

0 1 1 1 0 0 1 0 1 1 0 0 1 1 0 1 1 1 0 1 1 1 0 0 0 0 1 1 1 0 0 0 1 0 1 1 1

0 0 1 0 0 0 0 0 0 1 0 1 1 0 1]

Input [2]:

plt.scatter(Data[:,0], Data[:,1], c = db.labels_)

plt.xlabel(db.labels_[0])

plt.ylabel(db.labels_[1])

plt.hold

plt.show

Output [2]:

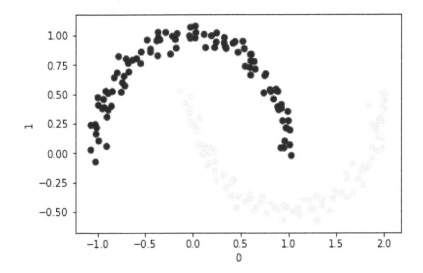

Prediction of Moons Dataset using DBSCAN

Sure enough, the performance of the DBSCAN clustering is best among all clustering algorithms. It has made many clear clusters as compared to K-means clustering and Agglomerative clustering. Although it has used StandardScaler, it has still performed well in dividing the classes.

Rounding off clustering:

We have seen various methods of clustering and how these can help us achieve significant results. Some of these have are quicker while others are more accurate. We have gone through a few visual representations to see exactly how each of these work and how they produce results accordingly.

In the next chapter, we will be looking at how we can work with data that contains text. We will go through sentiment analysis with appropriate examples, we will look at what 'stopwords' are and how we can use methods to analyze the text to fetch desired results.

Chapter 5: Working with Text Data

We have discussed two types of features to represent our dataset. One type comprises a continuous feature that describes the quantity, and the other one is a categorical feature that represents items from fixed list. There is another type of data, which is text. Text data has many applications all over the world.

We have discussed one example of the email message in the 2nd chapter, in which we discussed that email messages could be an example of classification in which one has to classify the email as genuine or spam. The classification will be performed using the provided data. In fact, that email message might contain textual data, which is represented as strings. Similarly, if someone wants to learn about the opinion of any politician on any specific topic, we can take help from his/her speeches or tweets related to that topic to come to a conclusion. That speech or tweets will also contain some textual data that can further help us acquire a better understanding.

In a similar way, in case of customer services, a company needs to check whether the customer has lodged a complaint or an inquiry. This can be done by the representative of the company after checking the subject line of the email that has been sent by the customer. The subject line alone should provide a clue as to what nature of email the customer has sent. One can easily classify it as a complaint or inquiry. That email or document will also contain some textual data.

There are many scenarios in which we deal with textual data, and therefore we need to understand how to deal with textual data. We can perform some machine learning methods to perform classification, clustering or regression depending on these specific problems.

Types of Data Represented as Strings

Text in any dataset consists of strings, but it does not mean that all string features will be assumed as text data. A feature containing strings can represent categorical features as well, which is why we first need to check the data to analyze the constituents of datasets. The string can be comprised of four types, such as text data, categorical data, structured string data and free strings that can be semantically mapped to categories.

Categorical data comes from a fixed list. For example, you have a list of colors such as 'red,' 'green,' 'pink,' 'purple,' 'orange,' 'brown,' 'yellow' and 'black' and you ask someone to select his favorite color from specific list. The person will then select his/her favorite color present within the specific list. Each color will be represented by a categorical variable. As there are eight colors, there should be eight categorical variables. If he/she sees more than eight variables, it will no longer be an example of Categorical data.

This can happen as any color like black was misspelled as blak or blac, and that will lead to the creation of two or more variables for a specific color. As these different variables are representing the same color, these variables can be mapped to the same category.

If the person's favorite color is not present in that specific list, it is either because the person is looking for an unusual color, or that person is confused between 'gray' or 'grey,' or the person can come up with names like 'midnight blue,' which are difficult to be mapped into any color. Depending on the response you get, if the said response does not belong to the primary list, it is considered to be a part of a secondary list. It will then be referred as free strings that can be semantically mapped to categories.

The other type is structured string data. It does not come from fixed categories. It contains structures such as names and addresses of people, telephone numbers, and dates. These types of data demand more effort to deal with.

Text data is the last type of string data that consists of phrases or sentences. This type contains examples of tweets, chats, and reviews. For text analysis, natural language processing (NLP) plays a vital role here.

Sentiment Analysis of Movie Reviews

Sentiment analysis has become a very popular field these days. We will apply sentiment analysis to movie reviews. Reviews comprise of either positive or negative feedback from the audience. The dataset is collected from the Internet Movie Database website. It contains text-based movie reviews.

You will need to download this dataset and then load it in Python. This dataset contains two folders, one is for training data, and the other one is the test data. Both of these folders are further divided into subfolders where one is 'pos' and the other one is 'neg'. The 'pos' folder contains positive reviews while the 'neg' folder contains negative reviews. The dataset is available at *http://ai.stanford.edu/~amaas/data/sentiment/*.

Input [1]:

Importing required libraries

from sklearn.datasets import load_files

import matplotlib.pyplot as plt

import numpy as np

Reading input Training data

```python
reviews_trn = load_files("aclImdb/train/")


# Extracting data and target values from Training data

Data_trn = reviews_trn.data

Target_trn = reviews_trn.target


print("Type of Data_trn: {}".format(type(Data_trn)))
```

Output [1]:

Type of Data_trn: <class 'list'>

Input [3]:

```python
print("Length of Data_trn: {}".format(len(Data_trn)))
```

Output [2]:

Length of Data_trn: 75000

Input [3]:

```python
print("Data_trn [1]:\n{}".format(Data_trn[1]))
```

Output [3]:

Data_trn [1]:

b"Amount of disappointment I am getting these days seeing movies like Partner, Jhoom Barabar and now, Heyy Babyy is gonna end my habit of seeing first day shows.

The movie is an utter disappointment because it had the potential to become a laugh riot only if the d\xc3\xa9butant director, Sajid Khan hadn't tried too many things. Only saving grace in the movie were the last thirty minutes, which were seriously funny elsewhere the movie fails miserably. First half was desperately been tried to look funny but wasn't. Next 45 minutes were emotional and looked totally artificial and illogical.

OK, when you are out for a movie like this you don't expect much logic but all the flaws tend to appear when you don't enjoy the movie and thats the case with Heyy Babyy. Acting is good but thats not enough to keep one interested.

For the positives, you can take hot actresses, last 30 minutes, some comic scenes, good acting by the lead cast and the baby. Only problem is that these things do not come together properly to make a good movie.

Anyways, I read somewhere that It isn't a copy of Three men and a baby but I think it would have been better if it was."

Input [4]:

```
Data_trn = [doc.replace(b"<br />", b" ") for doc in Data_trn]
print("Samples per class: {}".format(np.bincount(Target_trn)))
```

Output [4]:

Samples per class: [12500 12500 50000]

Input [5]:

```
# Reading input Test data
reviews_tst = load_files("data/aclImdb/test/")
# Extracting data and target values from Test data
Data_tst = reviews_tst.data
Target_tst = reviews_tst.target
```

```
print("Number       of       documents       in       test       data:
{}".format(len(Data_tst)))
```

Output [5]:

Number of documents in test data: 25000

Input [6]:

```
Data_tst = [doc.replace(b"<br />", b" ") for doc in Data_tst]

print("Samples per class (test):
{}".format(np.bincount(Target_tst)))
```

Output [6]:

Samples per class (test): [12500 12500]

Representing Text Data as Bags of Words

We already have discussed the importance of text data. The usage of bags of words for machine learning methods has become very popular. While dealing with this representation, we usually remove some of the structures, such as words, sentences, paragraphs, chapters, and formatting. It only counts words that appear in each text. By removing structure and counting just word, it provides a representation of text in the form of a 'bag.'

While carrying out a representation of bags of words, the steps required are as follows;

· Splitting each document into words that are known as tokens and the process, that is known as tokenization.

· The collection of vocabulary of all words appearing in each document and numbering them is known as vocabulary building.

· Counting words in vocabulary is known as encoding.

Applying Bag of Words on a Toy dataset

Bag of words is applied in CountVectorizor, which is used to perform transformation. We are applying bag of words to the toy dataset.

Input [1]:

```python
# Initializing words

words = ["Every one is not wise,","Every one can not be wise,"]


# Importing required libraries

from sklearn.feature_extraction.text import CountVectorizer

Cvect = CountVectorizer()

Cvect.fit(words)
```

Output [1]:

```
CountVectorizer(analyzer='word', binary=False,
decode_error='strict',
    dtype=<class 'numpy.int64'>, encoding='utf-8',
input='content',
    lowercase=True, max_df=1.0, max_features=None,
min_df=1,
    ngram_range=(1, 1), preprocessor=None,
stop_words=None,
    strip_accents=None, token_pattern='(?u)\\b\\w\\w+\\b',
    tokenizer=None, vocabulary=None)
```

Input [2]:

```
print("Size of Vocabulary: {}".format(len(Cvect.vocabulary_)))
```

Output [2]:

Size of Vocabulary: 7

Input [3]:

```
print("Content of Vocabulary:\n {}".format(Cvect.vocabulary_))
```

Output [3]:

Content of Vocabulary:

{'every': 2, 'one': 5, 'is': 3, 'not': 4, 'wise': 6, 'can': 1, 'be': 0}

You can observe the size of vocabulary and counts of each word in the list of words. It is showing the number of occurrences for each word.

If you want to get the bag of words representation of training data, you can use 'transform'.

Input [1]:

bag_of_words = Cvect.transform(words)

print("bag_of_words: {}".format(repr(bag_of_words)))

Output [1]:

bag_of_words: <2x7   sparse   matrix   of   type   '<class 'numpy.int64'>'

   with 11 stored elements in Compressed Sparse Row format>

You can observe the bag of words representation of training data. Bag of words representation is stored in SciPy sparse matrix which only stores non-zero entries. If you want to mapping of words you can perform below steps.

Input [2]:

print("Dense Representation of bag of words:\n{}".format(bag_of_words.toarray()))

Output [2]:

Dense Representation of bag of words:

[[0 0 1 1 1 1 1]

 [1 1 1 0 1 1 1]]

You can see that words have been mapped to either 0 or 1.

Applying Bag of Words on Movie Reviews

Input [1]:

Importing required libraries

from sklearn.datasets import load_files

from sklearn.feature_extraction.text import CountVectorizer

import matplotlib.pyplot as plt

import numpy as np

Reading input data

reviews_trn = load_files("aclImdb/train/")

reviews_tst = load_files("aclImdb/test/")

```python
# Extracting data and target values from Training data

Data_trn = reviews_trn.data

Target_trn = reviews_trn.target


# Extracting data and target values from Test data

Data_tst = reviews_tst.data

Target_tst = reviews_tst.target


Cvect = CountVectorizer()

Cvect.fit(Data_trn)


Data_trn = Cvect.transform(Data_trn)
print("Data_trn:\n{}".format(repr(Data_trn)))
```

Output [1]:

Data_trn:

<75000x124255 sparse matrix of type '<class 'numpy.int64'>'

with 10359806 stored elements in Compressed Sparse Row format>

You can check that the shape of Data_trn after bag of words representation is 75000 x 124255 with a vocabulary of 124,255. Once again, the Bag of words representation is stored in SciPy sparse matrix which only stores non-zero entries. If you want to get details of vocabulary, you can perform the following steps:

Input [1]:

```
names_feature = Cvect.get_feature_names()

print("Number of features: {}".format(len(names_feature)))
```

Output [1]:

Number of features: 124255

Input [2]:

```
print("First 20 features:\n{}".format(names_feature[:20]))
```

Output [2]:

First 20 features:

['00', '000', '0000',
'00000000000000000000000000000000001',
'0000000000001', '000000001', '000000003', '00000001',
'000001745', '00001', '0001', '00015', '0002', '0007', '00083',
'000ft', '000s', '000th', '001', '002']

Input [3]:

print("Features   from   50010   to
50030:\n{}".format(names_feature[50010:50030]))

Output [3]:

Features from 50010 to 50030:

['heatman', 'heatmiser', 'heaton', 'heats', 'heatseeker', 'heatwave',
'heave', 'heaved', 'heaven', 'heavenlier', 'heavenliness', 'heavenly',
'heavens', 'heavenward', 'heaves', 'heavier', 'heavies', 'heaviest',
'heavily', 'heaviness']

Input [4]:

```
print("Every                                              5000th
feature:\n{}".format(names_feature[::5000]))
```

Output [4]:

Every 5000th feature:

['00', 'aluin', 'banquière', 'brandie', 'chcialbym', 'corruptible', 'devagan', 'eisenburg', 'fetiches', 'ghar', 'heathen', 'indy', 'kerchner', 'locasso', 'meistersinger', 'narrators', 'overwhelmingly', 'portugese', 'recreating', 'samharris', 'silveira', 'stolen', 'themself', 'undeveloped', 'weidler']

We can observe that data is very big, and maybe some of it is useless, which is why we should apply a better feature extraction. We first need to apply classification so that we can compare its performance with one after removing some features.

Applying Logistic Regression on Movie Reviews

Input:

Importing required libraries

from sklearn.datasets import load_files

from sklearn.feature_extraction.text import CountVectorizer

from sklearn.model_selection import cross_val_score

```python
from sklearn.linear_model import LogisticRegression

import matplotlib.pyplot as plt

import numpy as np


# Reading input data

reviews_trn = load_files("aclImdb/train/")

reviews_tst = load_files("aclImdb/test/")


# Extracting data and target values from Training data

Data_trn = reviews_trn.data

Target_trn = reviews_trn.target


# Extracting data and target values from Test data

Data_tst = reviews_tst.data

Target_tst = reviews_tst.target


Cvect = CountVectorizer()
```

```
Cvect.fit(Data_trn)


Data_trn = Cvect.transform(Data_trn)


scores = cross_val_score(LogisticRegression(), Data_trn,
Target_trn, cv = 5)

print("Accuracy: {:.2f}".format(np.mean(scores)))
```

Output:

Accuracy: 0.71

Applying Logistic Regression with Gridsearch on Movie Reviews

Input:

```
# Importing required libraries

from sklearn.datasets import load_files

from sklearn.model_selection import cross_val_score
```

```python
from sklearn.linear_model import LogisticRegression

from sklearn.feature_extraction.text import CountVectorizer

from sklearn.model_selection import GridSearchCV

import matplotlib.pyplot as plt

import numpy as np


# Reading input data

reviews_trn = load_files("aclImdb/train/")

reviews_tst = load_files("aclImdb/test/")


# Extracting data and target values from Training data

Data_trn = reviews_trn.data

Target_trn = reviews_trn.target


# Extracting data and target values from Test data

Data_tst = reviews_tst.data

Target_tst = reviews_tst.target
```

```
Cvect = CountVectorizer()

Cvect.fit(Data_trn)


Data_trn = Cvect.transform(Data_trn)


prm_grd = {'C': [0.001, 0.01, 0.1, 1, 10]}

grd = GridSearchCV(LogisticRegression(), prm_grd, cv = 5)

grd.fit(Data_trn, Target_trn)

print("Cross validation score: {:.2f}".format(grd.best_score_))

print("Parameter with best performance: ", grd.best_params_)
```

Output:

Cross validation score: 0.72

Parameter with best performance: {'C' : 0.1}

You can observe that cross validation score using value of C = is achieved. We should check performance on test data as well which will further describe the performance of algorithm.

Input:

```
Data_tst = Cvect.transform(Target_tst)

print("{:.2f}".format(grd.score(Data_tst, Target_tst)))
```

Output:

0.70

We have checked the accuracies of logistic regression with and without GridSearch. We need to apply a better feature extraction here, as well. We should look to remove useless or less impactful features. It can be observed that we have used CountVectorizer, which converts all words to lowercase characters, which means 'Some', 'some" and sOme will correspond to the same token.

It is a good thing to have as some words can be mistakenly written in uppercase and can be differentiated with the same word in lowercase, but despite this feature of CountVectorizer, we have observed that there are still some useless features or words which need to be removed.

Stopwords

We can remove the useless words by using stopwords. It removes words that are repeated over and over again.

Input [1]:

```
# Importing required libraries

from sklearn.datasets import load_files

from sklearn.model_selection import cross_val_score

from sklearn.linear_model import LogisticRegression

from sklearn.feature_extraction.text import CountVectorizer

from sklearn.model_selection import GridSearchCV

import matplotlib.pyplot as plt

import numpy as np


# Reading input data

reviews_trn = load_files("aclImdb/train/")

reviews_tst = load_files("aclImdb/test/")
```

```python
# Extracting data and target values from Training data

Data_trn = reviews_trn.data

Target_trn = reviews_trn.target


# Extracting data and target values from Test data

Data_tst = reviews_tst.data

Target_tst = reviews_tst.target

Cvect = CountVectorizer(min_df = 5).fit(Data_trn)

X_train = Cvect.transform(Data_trn)

print("X_train with min_df: {}".format(repr(X_train)))
```

Output [1]:

X_train with min_df: <75000x124055 sparse matrix of type '<class 'numpy.int64'>'

with 10359846 stored elements in Compressed Sparse Row format>

We can observe that with demanding at least five occurrences, we have reduced features from 124255 to 124055, which means reduction of 200 features. Now we need to check the accuracy of logistic regression algorithm after reducing useless words.

Input [2]:

```
grd = GridSearchCV(LogisticRegression(), prm_grd, cv = 5)

grd.fit(Data_trn, Target_trn)

print("Cross validation score: {:.2f}".format(grd.best_score_))
```

Output [2]:

Cross validation score: 0.72

We can observe that even after reducing useless words, accuracy of logistic regression algorithm is unchanged. Although the accuracy has not improved, we have reduced the number of features by getting the same performance, which means we have done good by reducing words that are meaningless.

Applying Logistic Regression with Gridsearch and Stopwords on Movie Reviews

Input [1]:

```
# Importing required libraries

from sklearn.datasets import load_files

from sklearn.model_selection import cross_val_score

from sklearn.linear_model import LogisticRegression

from sklearn.feature_extraction.text import CountVectorizer

from sklearn.model_selection import GridSearchCV

import matplotlib.pyplot as plt

import numpy as np


# Reading input data

reviews_trn = load_files("aclImdb/train/")

reviews_tst = load_files("aclImdb/test/")


# Extracting data and target values from Training data
```

```
Data_trn = reviews_trn.data

Target_trn = reviews_trn.target


# Extracting data and target values from Test data

Data_tst = reviews_tst.data

Target_tst = reviews_tst.target


Cvect = CountVectorizer(min_df = 5, stop_words = "english").fit(Data_trn)

X_train = Cvect.transform(Data_trn)

print("X_train with stop words:\n{}".format(repr(X_train)))
```

Output [1]:

X_train with stop words:

<75000x123865 sparse matrix of type '<class 'numpy.int64'>'

with 10359836 stored elements in Compressed Sparse Row format>

We can again observe that with applying stopwords, we have reduced features from 124,055 to 123,865, which means a reduction of 190 features. Now, we need to check the accuracy of the logistic regression algorithm after the reduction.

Input [2]:

```
grd = GridSearchCV(LogisticRegression(), param_grid, cv = 5)

grd.fit(Data_trn, Target_trn)

print("Cross validation score: {:.2f}".format(grid.best_score_))
```

Output [2]:

Cross validation score: 0. 73

Applying Logistic Regression with tf-id Vectorizer and Stopwords on Movie Reviews

Input [1]:

```
# Importing required libraries

from sklearn.datasets import load_files
```

```python
from sklearn.model_selection import cross_val_score

from sklearn.linear_model import LogisticRegression

from sklearn.model_selection import GridSearchCV

from sklearn.feature_extraction.text import TfidfVectorizer

from sklearn.pipeline import make_pipeline

import matplotlib.pyplot as plt

import numpy as np


# Reading input data

reviews_trn = load_files("aclImdb/train/")

reviews_tst = load_files("aclImdb/test/")


# Extracting data and target values from Training data

Data_trn = reviews_trn.data

Target_trn = reviews_trn.target
```

Extracting data and target values from Test data

```
Data_tst = reviews_tst.data

Target_tst = reviews_tst.target

ppe = make_pipeline(TfidfVectorizer(min_df = 5, norm = None), LogisticRegression())

prm_grd = {'logisticregression__C': [0.001, 0.01, 0.1, 1, 10]}

grd = GridSearchCV(ppe, prm_grd, cv = 5)

grd.fit(Data_trn, Target_trn)

print("Cross validation score: {:.2f}".format(grd.best_score_))
```

Output [1]:

Cross validation score: 0.73

Applying Natural language toolkit on Email

We will be processing some emails now. We will first look at the original email and the one after some processing to get a better understanding. You can use any email and carry out the process on it.

Input [1]:

Importing required libraries

from nltk.stem import SnowballStemmer

import string

The first part is to give an appropriate path of the file and read the file.

d6=[]

d=open("2","r")

d1 = d.read()

Output [1]:

Message-ID: <26985403.1075859469480.JavaMail.evans@thyme>

Date: Wed, 26 Dec 2001 09:41:22 -0800 (PST)

From: susan.bailey@enron.com

To: stephanie.panus@enron.com

Subject: FW: People on Termination List

Cc: stewart.rosman@enron.com

Mime-Version: 1.0

Content-Type: text/plain; charset=us-ascii

Content-Transfer-Encoding: 7bit

Bcc: stewart.rosman@enron.com

X-From: Bailey, Susan
</O=ENRON/OU=NA/CN=RECIPIENTS/CN=SBAILE2>

X-To: Panus, Stephanie
</O=ENRON/OU=NA/CN=RECIPIENTS/CN=Spanus>

X-cc: Rosman, Stewart
</O=ENRON/OU=NA/CN=RECIPIENTS/CN=Srosman>

X-bcc:

X-Folder: \Susan_Bailey_Jan2002\Bailey, Susan\Deleted Items

X-Origin: Bailey-S

X-FileName: sbaile2 (Non-Privileged).pst

Stephanie,

Please add the following individuals set forth below to list of recipients to receive the Master Termination Log.

Also, please add Steve Hall to that list.

Thanks,

Susan

-----Original Message-----

From: Rosman, Stewart

Sent: Wednesday, December 26, 2001 11:37 AM

To: Bailey, Susan

Subject: People on Termination List

Sean Crandall

Diana Scholtes

Jeff Richter

Chris Mallory

Mark Fischer

Tom Alonso

Input [2]:

Once the contents are available in Python, the next step is to remove the metadata from the email.

the string 'X-FileName'. This string is present in every email and can be 'split'.

d2=d1.split('X-FileName')

Output [2]:

% First part of d2

Message-ID: <26985403.1075859469480.JavaMail.evans@thyme>

Date: Wed, 26 Dec 2001 09:41:22 -0800 (PST)

From: susan.bailey@enron.com

To: stephanie.panus@enron.com

Subject: FW: People on Termination List

Cc: stewart.rosman@enron.com

Mime-Version: 1.0

Content-Type: text/plain; charset=us-ascii

Content-Transfer-Encoding: 7bit

Bcc: stewart.rosman@enron.com

X-From: Bailey, Susan
</O=ENRON/OU=NA/CN=RECIPIENTS/CN=SBAILE2>

X-To: Panus, Stephanie
</O=ENRON/OU=NA/CN=RECIPIENTS/CN=Spanus>

X-cc: Rosman, Stewart
</O=ENRON/OU=NA/CN=RECIPIENTS/CN=Srosman>

X-bcc:

X-Folder: \Susan_Bailey_Jan2002\Bailey, Susan\Deleted Items

X-Origin: Bailey-S

% First part of d2

: sbaile2 (Non-Privileged).pst

Stephanie,

Please add the following individuals set forth below to list of recipients to receive the Master Termination Log.

Also, please add Steve Hall to that list.

Thanks,

Susan

-----Original Message-----

From: Rosman, Stewart

Sent: Wednesday, December 26, 2001 11:37 AM

To: Bailey, Susan

Subject: People on Termination List

Sean Crandall

Diana Scholtes

Jeff Richter

Chris Mallory

Mark Fischer

Tom Alonso

Input [3]:

Once the email body is retrieved, the next step is to remove punctuation, and split the text into individual words.

for c in string.punctuation:

    d3= d2[1].replace(c,"")

d4=d3.split(' ')

Output [3]:

% d3

: sbaile2 (Non-Privileged).pst

Stephanie,

Please add the following individuals set forth below to list of recipients to receive the Master Termination Log.

Also, please add Steve Hall to that list.

Thanks,

Susan

-----Original Message-----

From: Rosman, Stewart

Sent: Wednesday, December 26, 2001 11:37 AM

To: Bailey, Susan

Subject: People on Termination List

Sean Crandall

Diana Scholtes

Jeff Richter

Chris Mallory

Mark Fischer

Tom Alonso

% d4

:

sbaile2

(Non-Privileged).pst

Stephanie,

Please

add

the

following

individuals

set

forth

below

to

list

of

recipients

to

receive

the

Input [4]:

Now apply SnowballStemmer on each word. [hint: use .append() method to make a continual list of words]

stemmer = SnowballStemmer("english")

for i in range(len(d4)):

   d5=stemmer.stem(d4[i])

      d6.append (d5)

The resulting list of words is then 'joined' again into a single string.

d6 = " ".join(d6)

Output [4]:

% d5

alonso

% d6

: sbaile2 (non-privileged).pst

stephanie,

pleas add the follow individu set forth below to list of recipi to receiv the master termin log.

also, pleas add steve hall to that list.

thanks,

susan

-----origin message-----

from: rosman, stewart

sent: wednesday, decemb 26, 2001 11:37 am

to: bailey, susan

subject: peopl on termin list

sean crandall

diana scholtes

jeff richter

chri mallory

mark fischer

tom alonso

In the above example, we have successfully processed an email. We began with an email that contained far too much information, most of which we were neither interested in nor looking forward to.

We then processed the same email and removed meta descriptions and other unnecessary words to bring out only the information we were interested in. The end result is an information extracted from the email that is relevant and needed.

While this process is lengthy, it does beg the question, why would you do all that when you can copy and paste the email body yourself? Remember, we are undergoing Machine learning and naturally, we are expecting to deal with a bulk of data. There is every likelihood that you will not be dealing with data that is only comprising of a single email. By training the model to filter out unnecessary information for hundreds of thousands of email in the shortest span of time, you are saving yourself quite a lot of process. The machine will now be able to carry out the same for you instead, at a rate far quicker than an individual can deliver.

To conclude this chapter, we have learned how to handle data that comprises of text. Unlike previous chapters, where we were manipulating numeric values and methods to plot graphs and visualize the data, this chapter dealt with 'strings' of text as you would normally find in emails and movie reviews.

Major organizations use sentiment analysis to tailor recommendations using this information for the members of the general audience. Through using such methods and algorithms, we can train the model of the machine to learn and store words as 'vocabulary' and then ensure that the machine can use these to gain valuable data and analyze the same. Through effective analysis, we can have quite a lot of work carried out in the least timeframe possible.

In the final chapter, we will be looking at the real world applications of Machine learning. While there are quite a lot of these in existence, we will only be focusing on a select few to provide data scientists and machine learners a better understanding of the applications in the real world.

Chapter 6: Machine Learning Real World Applications

Machine learning is an all-important field throughout the world. Its application can be seen in many apps, software, and research-based projects of various magnitudes. Machine learning has been around for quite some time now; however, recently it has garnered a massive attention from the worldwide audience and computer experts.

It can be used in medical fields for diagnosing various diseases using classification or regression methods, within social networks to locate your friends, get suggestions and a feed that is tailor-made for your liking, and in forecasting weather conditions by providing the model with a number of features that can further train and classify, predict or forecast weather when required. It is capable of processing extensively large data for large organizations or small-sized data for smaller organizations as well.

Where can you use machine learning?

We can use machine learning in many applications when it comes to the real world. Before we go ahead, let us quickly stroll through the previous examples discussed to remind ourselves of some practical examples. Then, we shall look at four more large-scale uses of machine learning. For this book, we will not be covering small scale usage of machine learning. After all, we are trying to learn to be a part of a bigger picture.

In the beginning, we discussed how the spam filter used a list of blacklisted words which helped the filter to identify spam words or emails. This filter can be used as one of the examples of intelligent applications. This problem can be solved by a human as well, but in that case, a person requires thorough understanding of processes in order to come up with such a model. Manual or hand-coded rules can be useful but not in every case.

Similarly, in another example we learned that the hand-coded method fails in a specific aspect, and that is the detection of a face in an image. Although every smartphone these days can detect and identify faces in the pictures, this was far from possible in the past. The reason behind failure in detection and identification of faces in an image in the recent past is due to the difference in perception of pixels between a human and a computer.

Apart from these, The application of machine learning can be seen across various sectors of our daily lives. These include and are not limited to the following:

1. Financial institutions – Financial institutions like banks have greatly benefited from machine learning and have used machine learning to create complex algorithms to learn and identify suspicious or fraudulent transactions. There were times when a transaction could not be identified at such a rapid pace and most of the people who carried out these illegal activities got away with it. Now, things are different. With large processing power and memory available for the systems of today, financial institutions can run transactions through a trained model and immediately identify if any transaction, regardless of how genuine it looks, is flagged as suspicious or fraudulent. These transaction checks have greatly improved the leakages in reserves and allowed the world to host better banking systems where the money and financial records remain safe and secure, away from prying eyes.

2. Sentiment Analysis – Major streaming platforms across the globe, such as Netflix and Amazon Prime, are using sentiment analysis to analyze the behavior of the user and learn of what the user might like or dislike. This saves quite a lot of time and guess work as the entire profile is categorized by labels such as likes, dislikes, and only then recommendations are proposed for the users. This creates a high chance that the user might end up clicking on the said recommendation. This isn't just limited to streaming services, many other websites use the same approach, such as Facebook, twitter and many more. This is why you normally end up getting feeds that are more likely to engage you.

3. Healthcare – We have looked at a few variations of machine learning methods using Iris and Breast Cancer datasets. However, the reason we used those is because machine learning plays a vital role in the health sector. With top-notch machineries, equipment and analysis tools, machine learning provides ground-breaking results in the least amount of time imaginable. What was once done in days can now be done within minutes. No longer do you need to consult various doctors regarding a scan just to find out the condition of your ailment. Now, the clever machines and models continue to evolve and learn to decode the films and scans to predict the answers with amazing accuracy. The bright side is, this field will continue to use machine learning for generations to come.

4. E-Commerce – Sure enough, businesses that operate online, such as Amazon, eBay, Alibaba, use machine learning to understand the buying patterns, wishlisted items and items the users might browse through to come up with recommendations. For any business person, it is imperative to propose or recommend items which have a high likelihood of being sold to a specific type of customer. Through machine learning, that is being done every single minute of every day. The more you browse such e-commerce websites, the more data they compile to refine their accuracy in recommending products. Eventually, you will be spoiled for choice as these recommendations, almost all of them, will be too tempting to resist. The fact of the matter

is that these existed within the website before as well, the only difference is, you may have skipped past these. Now, since the machine has learned of your shopping behavior and the kind of items you are interested in, the model will propose the ones which are most likely to be sold to you.

The world continues to evolve and with it the data that is being collected. Every day we spend hours on our cell phones and computers, scrolling through websites, products and even social media pages. This data is growing larger and larger for every single one of us. Imagine the amount of data that exists on the internet now. Processing that will require hundreds of years, if not thousands, if done by human beings.

Machine learning has drastically changed everything for us and taken over the arduous task of carrying out such large operations in unbelievably short span of time. Not only does that save us time, it saves us quite a lot of effort and possibly money as well. Now, we can create our own models and use the data we have gathered to tailor the kind of recommendations we would like the customers to see, effectively increasing our chances for great sales.

Before we end the chapter, below are some working data using a few more datasets. Have a look through and try to find out what is being done here. You can try and alter the variables, the methods and see how that would affect the overall output of the same.

Applying Machine Learning methods on Wine Data

Input [1]:

```python
# Importing required libraries

import pandas as pd

from sklearn.cluster import KMeans

from sklearn.preprocessing import StandardScaler

from sklearn.pipeline import make_pipeline


df = pd.read_csv('wine_data.csv')


samples = df.iloc[:, 2: 10].values

model = KMeans(n_clusters = 3)

labels = model.fit_predict(samples)


ct = pd.crosstab(labels,df['class_name'])

print("Crosstab with simple Kmeans:\n",ct)
```

Output [1]:

Crosstab with simple Kmeans:

class_name	Barbera	Barolo	Grignolino
row_0			
0	5	15	6
1	19	9	46
2	24	35	19

	class_label	alcohol	...	od280	proline
count	178.000000	178.000000	...	178.000000	178.000000
mean	1.938202	13.000618	...	2.611685	746.893258
std	0.775035	0.811827	...	0.709990	314.907474
min	1.000000	11.030000	...	1.270000	278.000000
25%	1.000000	12.362500	...	1.937500	500.500000
50%	2.000000	13.050000	...	2.780000	673.500000
75%	3.000000	13.677500	...	3.170000	985.000000
max	3.000000	14.830000	...	4.000000	1680.000000

Input [2]:

```
print(df.describe())


scaler = StandardScaler()

scaler.fit(samples)

scaled_samples = scaler.transform(samples)

# Applying KMeans and pd.crosstab on the scaled_samples

Model = KMeans(n_clusters = 3)

labels = model.fit_predict(scaled_samples)

ct = pd.crosstab(labels,df['class_name'])

print("Crosstab with StandardScaler and Kmeans:\n",ct)
```

Output [2]:

[8 rows x 14 columns]

Crosstab with StandardScaler and Kmeans:

 class_name Barbera Barolo Grignolino

row_0

	0	55	4
0			
1	46	0	13
2	2	4	54

Input [3]:

#%% Pipeline

Scaler = StandardScaler()

Kmeans = KMeans(n_clusters = 3)

pipeline = make_pipeline(scaler,kmeans)

pipeline.fit(samples)

labels = pipeline.predict(samples)

ct = pd.crosstab(labels,df['class_name'])

print("Crosstab with pipeline:\n",ct)

Output [3]:

Crosstab with pipeline:

class_name	Barbera	Barolo	Grignolino
row_0			
0	1	5	44
1	47	0	22
2	0	54	5

Applying Machine Learning methods on Banknote Authentication Data

Input [1]:

```
# Importing required libraries

from sklearn.model_selection import train_test_split

import pandas as pd

from sklearn.tree import DecisionTreeClassifier

from matplotlib import pyplot as plt

file = pd.read_csv('bank_note.txt')
```

```python
data = file.values

x = data[: , 0:4]

y = data[: , 4]



#Data Splitting

x_train, x_test, y_train, y_test = train_test_split(x, y, test_size
= 0.3,

                                    random_state = 15)



clf = DecisionTreeClassifier(criterion = 'gini',
min_samples_split = 65,

                            max_features = 3,
                            max_depth = 150)

clf.fit(x_train,y_train)

out = clf.predict(x_test)

acc = (sum(out == y_test))/len(out)

print('Accuracy of the classifier is {:.4f}'.format(acc*100))
```

```
#Data Plotting

plt.plot(x_train[y_train == 0,0],x_train[y_train ==
0,1],'rs',label = 'Original')

plt.hold

plt.plot(x_train[y_train == 1,0],x_train[y_train ==
1,1],'g.',label='Fake')

plt.legend()

plt.xlabel('variance of Wavelet Transformed image')

plt.ylabel('skewness of Wavelet Transformed image')


plt.figure(2)

plt.plot(x_train[y_train == 0,2],x_train[y_train ==
0,3],'rs',label = 'Original')

plt.hold

plt.plot(x_train[y_train == 1,2],x_train[y_train ==
1,3],'g.',label = 'Fake')

plt.legend()

plt.xlabel('curtosis of Wavelet Transformed image ')

plt.ylabel('entropy of image')
```

Output [1]:

Accuracy of the classifier is 93.4466

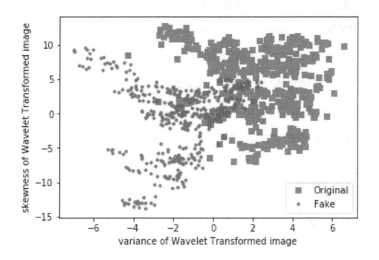

Prediction of first two features of Banknote Dataset using Decision Tree Classifier

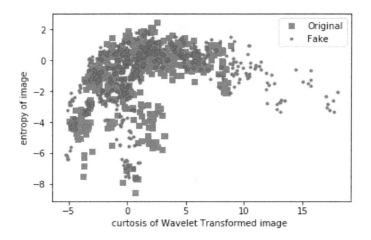

Prediction of last two features of Banknote Dataset using Decision Tree Classifier

Both of these datasets are collected from https://archive.ics.uci.edu/ml/datasets.php. You can use this repository to download and use any dataset you might like. It is recommended that you continue practicing your codes and machine learning by downloading various machine learning datasets. These will help you grasp the concepts far better than just repeating everything the book has to offer.

Conclusion

Admittedly, the book comprises of quite a few codes, all of which may seem daunting and rather overwhelming at first. If you have a good understanding of the Python programming language, you should easily be able to relate to the code and understanding what is being done at a certain given point. While our main objective was to ensure we visit some of the more technically advanced approaches and test out various models, check their accuracy and put them to work, we cannot deny that at the heart of the entire Machine Learning lies Python; a beautiful and intriguing language that continues to amaze the world.

In the start of this book, we looked upon various components, went through some details and established that this book caters to people with a good knowledge of Python and other important libraries. The purpose of this book was to allow you to seek out further datasets, libraries and components which would allow you to enhance your Machine Learning skills by using practical, real world examples.

We then discussed many machine learning methods and their applications as well. We also learned that machine learning can be divided into two types, supervised machine learning and unsupervised machine learning. Supervised machine learning contains the information of output label. Supervised machine learning is further split into two types, classification, and regression. Classification is used to predict discrete labels while regression is used to predict continuous numbers or floating-point numbers.

Classification is further divided into two categories, binary classification and multi-classification. Binary classification divides two classes while multi-classification separates multiple classes. In other words, we can say that binary classification provides either a yes or no as an answer. We discussed the example of classification of emails as an example of binary classification.

We also visited examples of regression such as prediction of an individual's annual income from his/her education, age and other related 'features' where predicted output will be an amount of any value. The predicted output can be any number, varying on the kind of data provided.

Unsupervised machine learning does not contain the information of the output label. It applies multiple methods including Euclidean distance. It contains k-means, agglomerative and DBSCAN methods which divide the datasets without knowing the information of output label.

Multiple methods of each category have been applied. We observed that linear kernel worked better than other kernels in classification. Some methods worked well by increasing the value of C while others performed well by reducing the value of tolerance.

We also observed that we should limit the number of features while training and predicting output otherwise we can lead to lack of accuracy.

We observed that K-means clustering performed well but in simple problems. For problems which were complex in nature, it failed.

Agglomerative and DBSCAN methods performed better than K-means clustering, especially in difficult cases. We also observed that many scales can be used to increase the efficiency of algorithms. It was also shown that many scales can be used as preprocessing especially before applying classification as some methods are sensitive to scales and perform well with application of scales such as SVM and NN.

Finally, we analyzed some text data and were successfully able to remove unnecessary data from the said email while retaining the one that we require the most.

While the book has left out hundreds of other applications of machine learning, and thousands of datasets which could have been used, it is done deliberately to allow the aspiring learners to carry out experimentations and come up with better solutions through effective approach and model training.

Where possible, the links were shared so that you can gain access to such training model datasets.

Machine learning has gained quite a pace and promises to be a worthy field of interest for those willing to pursue a career in it. We have barely uncovered the tip of the iceberg, there is quite a lot remaining that we might not know yet. Machine learning will soon revolutionize ad impact quite a lot of things, which makes this the perfect time to get into some practice and start making your way to the top.

While you can continue to read various books and scroll through a gazillion videos available all over the internet, the best way to master machine learning is to implement the codes and try writing new ones. Come up with genuine ideas by visualizing a scenario and then focusing on the task. Learn and then teach the same to the model by supplying the appropriate data. The end results will always bring out something unique each time.

Great programmers and inventors have gone through extensive trial and error methods to come up with contributions which have helped the society, if not the world. However, you hold a distinct advantage over such success stories; they relied on man hours while you now have a machine to carry out the same extensive work but in a fraction of the time you may have taken otherwise. Use the knowledge and use it well!

Remember, there is no such thing as being "too late to learn." All it needs is commitment and a will to learn. Great inventors used the same age-old principles to come up with brilliant, ground-breaking inventions. Do not let the thought of being late to begin learning something new get to you. Your creativity is yours, and you are unique in your own way. With the knowledge you have gathered, let your creativity flow and practice. Who knows, you might very well be the next great mind to rise.

Let Machine Learning help you achieve great new success. This field holds significant potential and the future is only looking to grow bigger. Despite all the competition, despite the sheer number of aspiring students and masters, there is much to be done in this world to help others and create a more safe, secure and efficient environment. All it takes is one brilliant idea to change everything.

Whether you wish to bring a revolutionary new model to analyze blood samples, or detect fraudulent online transactions, you have all the time in the world to come up with something truly unique.

The beauty about the entire Machine Learning process is that you can explore far greater and more promising opportunities for yourself. The field is quite vast and you can get into various projects and institutions. Here are a few of the top ones which use or need Machine Learning:

1. Virtual Assistants - We are referring to technologies like Siri for iPhones. The world of voice recognition and virtual assistants is rapidly evolving. Now, even the television remote controls come with voice assistance. Machine learning plays an important part to make these applications successful. By gathering the data of your selection, your voice samples, and your day-to-day commands, you start getting more personalized recommendations and outputs. This is just the start; there is a long way to go as the world has just started getting used to such virtual assistants.

2. Face tracking - Whether you use facial recognition apps for surveillance purposes or for cinematography, face tracking requires complex algorithms to train the model in order to learn what face it needs to track and how to keep its focus on the subject of choice. We are still in early days which is why there is quite a lot to be done in this field as well. The applications will further diversify the use of machine learning in CCTVs, surveillance, video making, aerial/drone imaging and much more.

3. Search engine queries - We have already seen how search engines tend to immediately understand what we

are trying to search. Now, you know how! They use algorithms to try and understand the behavior of the user and identify what the user is trying to search for. Using features like their geographical location, age, and browsing habits, the search engines present results tailor-made for them.

4. Customer support - This might be a bit of a surprise, but the fact of the matter is that not always do you get to speak to a live customer service representative. There are quite a few occurrences where you will end up speaking to a 'bot' that is collecting the data and understanding what you are trying to find out. Using the abundant resources from the page, the bot will present the information to you accordingly while trying to gauge the exact nature of the query. This is far from perfect which is why if you can come up with an accurate model, you might be just moments away from becoming the next success story.

5. Traffic updates - Have you ever accessed the maps on your smartphone and come across warnings that the road you are travelling on is experiencing delays and severe traffic jams? Have you ever wondered how come

your cell phone knows that? Using GPS satellites, the number of phones or GPS modules installed within cars, the speed at which they travel, the machines immediately compute if the road is facing blocks or letting the traffic flow easily. The problem is that not many GPS modules are active or installed, which does kind of create discrepancies and there is a certain lag within the actual situation and the data that it represents on the screen. While there is Machine Learning already at play, it does need upgrading. There is quite a lot of room for improvement and even new models to come and replace the old ones.

Finally, Machine Learning is still in its genesis. While the concept has lurked around for quite some time, it is only recently that things have truly started to manifest and bring forth successful stories and results. The applications go far beyond health care and financial institutions. The world awaits new ideas, there is always someone out there looking for a person of your caliber, understanding and knowledge. Train yourself by practicing and be the next success story; or better yet, train your machine to be one for you!

Bibliography

1.   Muller, A, C. & Guido, S. (2017). Introduction to Machine Learning with Python. Sebastopol, CA: O'Reilly Media Inc.

2.   Raschka, S. (2015). Python Machine Learning. Birmingham, UK: Packt Publishing Ltd.

3.   Heyy   Babyy,   Retrieved   10/2019,   from, https://www.imdb.com/title/tt0806088/reviews

4. Large Movie Review Dataset, Retrieved, 10/2019 from. http://ai.stanford.edu/~amaas/data/sentiment/

www.ingramcontent.com/pod-product-compliance
Lightning Source LLC
Chambersburg PA
CBHW071108050326
40690CB00008B/1157